A New Way to Be

BECOMING **RESILIENT**
ONE HABIT, BREATH, AND MOMENT AT A TIME

SOUL SEED
LEGACY·HOUSE

A New Way to Be

BECOMING **RESILIENT**
ONE HABIT, BREATH, AND MOMENT AT A TIME

MONICA BODURKA

To my amazing husband, Aubrey,
who not only embraced all the concepts in this book,
but actually helped create and build the programs
upon which this book is based.
I am so grateful to have you in my life.

And to my mother—my rock.

Contents

Introduction 1

PART ONE. BUILD YOUR FOUNDATION

A Fresh Take on Resilience 11
Critical Success Factors on Your Journey to Resilience 27
The Overwhelm Audit 35
Neuroscience Is Your Best Friend 47

PART TWO. KEYSTONES OF RESILIENCE

RESILIENCE KEYSTONE I—PHYSICAL MASTERY............................71

Sleep Deep 75
Eat Consciously.................................... 99
Move Often..................................... 119
Breathe Slowly 141

RESILIENCE KEYSTONE II—SELF-AWARENESS 157

Be Mindful / Be Present 161
Generate Positivity 189
Connect Authentically (and with Discernment) 213
Rest and Recharge................................ 227

RESILIENCE KEYSTONE III—INTENTIONAL ORIENTATION.... 243

Live with Intention 247
Strengthen Your Spirit 281

PART THREE. THE JOURNEY CONTINUES

Conclusion 299
Acknowlegments 303
Resources 305

Introduction

Become aware that there are no accidents
in our intelligent universe.
Realize that everything that shows up in your life
has something to teach you.
Appreciate everyone and everything.

—WAYNE DYER

It was a dreary day in late November 2020, over a year after my fall. I was nearing the end of my long neurology appointment. I had just finished completing my eye exercises and having my vagus nerve stimulated with a funny little device the super friendly, masked nurse placed on my tongue, behind my ears, and over my eyes.

It was the height of the Covid-19 pandemic. Although the kids were back at school, stores and restaurants were closed, and we all were doing that strange six-feet-apart social-distancing dance. The heaviness of fear, canceled holidays, and social isolation were in the air.

The neurologist came in to see how my symptoms were fairing under the treatment. The nurse and I were having a good laugh about something, as usual. He watched me perplexed as I shared that my symptoms were unchanged. I continued to have daily headaches and was very easily overstimulated, whether that be by light, sound, the smallest stressor, my computer, grocery stores, driving, TV, etc. The worst, I shared, was the insomnia that would not let up no matter what sleep hygiene habits I seemed to implement.

I had now been attending this clinic twice a week for over two months, and he and his staff had gotten to know me. In some ways, I enjoyed coming in. Frankly, it was social, and there were not many outlets for any social interaction at the time now that all Toronto stores were closed, an unimaginable occurrence before the holidays.

He looked at me, leaned in, and quietly asked, "Why aren't you depressed?"

I looked up at the neurologist, surprised. "Ah . . . should I be?"

"I'd say over ninety percent of my concussion patients, especially those with acute traumatic brain injuries like yours, are depressed. Some debilitating so."

I took a minute to collect my thoughts. It's true, since my fall over a year ago, I'd been battling severe headaches and insomnia. Light was torture and sound a huge stimulator of my fight and flight response. I couldn't work on my computer, much less scroll down my phone. TV was a no-no. The florescent lights of a grocery store were too much for me. In fact, any stimulus was nausea-creating—my hands would shake, my head would pound, I couldn't sleep, and not surprisingly, I was unable to function very well in the world.

I still remember the sound of my skull bashing against the pavement and my daughters screaming. We'd just returned from my in-laws' cottage. I was frenzied by the amount I had to do to prepare for a workshop I was running the next day—get dinner on, unpack, and get groceries for lunches the next day—but my girls wanted to play with their new "toys."

"Mama, come play with us, pleeeassse," they sang out and my guilt complex set in. I agreed.

As an aside, never get a ripstik for your kids! It is essentially a toy from hell. Imagine a skateboard with swivel wheels. They are absolutely dangerous. In fact, they have a funny warning on them: "No adults." Ha! Well, I didn't listen. On this warm and sunny day, my girls asked me to ride one down a concrete hill in the alleyway behind our home. While I had them wearing helmets, I wore none. It took me less than thirty seconds to catapult backward, helmet-less head onto a cement road at full speed.

Time. Stood. Still.

When the clock resumed, a year and a half later, I was still paying the price for my frenzied agreement to override my instincts and always put everyone, especially my precious girls, ahead of me.

The doctor waited for my answer. Now the nurse was curious and leaned in as well.

"It's true," I shared. "I am not depressed. Emotionally, I am frustrated. I often feel scared why the pain and insomnia are not letting up and what that means in the long term, but I feel strangely light. Dare I say, 'fine' despite the symptoms."

He rephrased the question. "What are you doing to keep mentally and psychologically strong?"

I smiled at the irony considering he was the expert. "I'm earning my resilience badge, and the concussion is my teacher," I said. "In other words, I believe that this has happened FOR me, not to me."

"Huh?" He looked perplexed.

Just before my fall, I shared, as part of my business as a health and well-being educator and coach for executives and coaches, I designed and launched a 10-week resilience program for overwhelmed professionals struggling with stress, burnout, and anxiety. The program, Resilient by Design, was about creating positive, sustainable habits that enabled participants to become healthier, happier, and stronger.

BCC (before concussion and Covid), I found myself not always following my own research and advice. Mentally, I knew the content, data, and best practices and could recite them all with great passion and fortitude but often did not follow my own advice. One could accuse me of being a bit of a fraud. However, when I fell, I gave my head a shake (literally), and I realized I could no longer operate the way I could before.

Not knowing what else to do to heal, I started to truly live my Resilient by Design program daily. I was forced to embody the practices. I started each day with a mediation in bed, then continued to my daily yoga morning practice that focused on breathing into my udana region (my neck and head) and calming my central nervous system. I cut out caffeine, sugar, and alcohol. I walked every single day. Midday, I meditated again and did a pranayama breathing practice. I went on a strict anti-inflammatory diet. I set boundaries like a rock star for the first time in my life. I said no to "opportunities." I listened to my body and the whispers of my soul—much easier to do when forced to embrace silence. I did all I could to be super mindful (so I didn't push beyond my pain threshold). I looked at my ego and self-identity, which was really acting up as I could not work at the same capacity as I used to. I became more self-aware. I cut out the news (not an easy task during a pandemic) and embraced stand-up comedy. Laughter is great medicine for the mind, body, and soul, and I could listen to it, release some positive endorphins, and not have to stimulate my eyes watching it.

I also, perhaps most importantly, changed my mindset from victim to owner of the situation. Seeing the concussion as a teacher or even a gift, I became interested to learn as opposed to feel broken.

My amazing yoga teachers always say, **"Do the practice and something will happen."**

Well, it did. And slowly I became a new person—a gentler, more compassionate, happier one. In fact, I noticed I was not as frazzled. I was more centered, more grounded, and *more resilient* to adversity than when I was teaching my resilience programs.

This book is not about how to deal with a concussion or to heal from one. To be honest, I continue to struggle with post-concussion symptoms at times, just not as acutely. Clearly, my learning is not done.

Rather, this book is about embodying resilience. We live in stressful times; we have been indoctrinated to believe that stress is somehow correlated with success. I know subconsciously I thought if I was busy and stressed that meant I was important.

If you feel you are frazzled and spinning or at your wits' end, please join me on this journey. Don't wait for burnout, a sickness, or an accident like I did. **This book is about remapping the inner networks of your brain to become a new you—a more resilient, happier, and healthier you.** A you that is okay, despite the hectic world around you. In my program live sessions, I like to say, "The bumps on the road will always be there, and often we don't foresee them, but the ride can still feel strangely smooth if you build your shock absorbers."

This road to becoming resilient can feel bumpy too. Creating new neuropathways in the brain takes time, effort, and strong motivation (which we call your WHY). But it is possible and so worth it. I am honored to embark on this journey together to hopefully make the road not only smoother, but also pleasant.

HOW THIS BOOK WORKS

This book is your guide to embodying resilience. Although there are stories and evidence-based research, the aim is to have you implement the practices and repeat them often enough to develop new neuropathways and a new you. After each chapter you will have a challenge exercise. Most of the time it is to "do the work and be resilient." Specifically, I will ask you to identify one micro practice you can implement from the habits presented. In our programs, we either meet once a week or the content is dripped weekly online. The program design makes it so that you have a week to implement the micro habit of choice. In a book format, the choice is yours. You can turn this into your own 10-week program and read a chapter at the beginning of the week, then use the week to implement the practice.

Frankly, that doesn't work for me. I am more of a "if I am into the book, I will read it all at once" kind of girl. Where I have tried to manage myself and read only one part at a time, I tended to forget about the book all together and move on to another one of the ten books on my bedside table. You know your preferences and tendencies; therefore, I suggest you choose your own adventure. The only caveat is that I highly recommend (insist, if I may) to not just read for empirical knowledge or entertainment purposes but to actually implement the practices. **We change ourselves by DOING**

even a little, not by knowing a lot. Just for fun, use yourself like a personal laboratory. See what happens when you start engaging practically with the content.

I also suggest, if you do read the whole thing at once, to go back and implement the habits one week at a time. There is magic in creating micro habits. First, they don't stress you out or trigger your central nervous system like making massive behavior change. Next, adding even just one tiny habit over time can create a massive compound effect. We will talk about this later.

Finally, please use the QR code at the back of the book to visit our website and the book resource web page. There you can find the challenge exercises, assessments, bonuses such as a guide to clean eating, and additional learning material by topic to help you dive deeper into all the areas of resilience.

Take my hand and let's do this together, one micro habit, breath, and moment at a time.

PART ONE.
BUILD YOUR FOUNDATION

Chapter 1

A FRESH TAKE ON RESILIENCE

You can't stop the waves, but you can learn to surf.
—Jon Kabat-Zinn

I used to not like the word "resilience." It sounded to me like being gritty or a grinding toughness that I did not resonate with. I am a Pisces after all, and apparently because of the position of the sun on the day I was born, I am soft-natured not tough.

I now teach how to cultivate resilience in self and others and am amazed how often people also think resilient means brutal hardness. In fact, at one workshop, a participant got up and shared his perspective. He said, "Resilience is about being able to take the hits in life and still remain standing." He then quoted Rocky (Sylvester Stallone's character) from the movie *Rocky Balboa*: "You, me, or nobody is gonna hit as hard as life. But it ain't how hard you hit. It's about how hard you can get hit and keep moving forward. How much you can take and keep moving forward."

I couldn't stop him from reciting the full quote. Clearly, he was inspired but also looked worn and desperate. I shared that unfortunately his definition is what leads to burnout and is not resilience.

Other participants said things like their grandmother was resilient because she lived through the tragedies of war. We would call that survival instinct, and thankfully, we all have that innately built in within us.

Resilience is NOT having the sh*t beaten out of us and still being able to stand upright.

Sure, resilience is the ability to recover quickly from adversities and a certain toughness. But in my courses, I share that resilience is also much more. It is like having built-in shock absorbers in a car or bicycle. Let me explain. We do not control the bumps in the road, and often we cannot even predict when they will be there. Covid, for example, was a big bump that we didn't see coming. But some people were able to glide across that experience with seeming ease and grace. The road was not as "bumpy" for them, and I would postulate that they, with or without knowing it, had cultivated these shock absorbers.

Another way of looking at it is to think of resilience as a fully charged battery. When adversity strikes or when there is an onslaught of stress, you can handle it with more grace when you are fully charged and well maintained. We all know that when you are constantly "on" you get depleted. If something unexpected were to happen, you may have no reserve and can fall apart or burn out.

We will spend a whole chapter on fully unplugging to build resilience. For now, think about whether you run on empty, like I did before concussing my brain. Also, ponder for a moment what really restores your battery, and whether you do it regularly.

Resilience also means the ability to spring back into shape, having elasticity, or as we often hear, the ability to bounce back post adversity. I agree with (and research demonstrates) that flexibility is a key component of resilience. I like to use analogies, and here I often show an image of a beautiful bamboo forest. Bamboo is such a great example. Not only because of the speed and grace it grows with but that it doesn't break under pressure. I once watched a YouTube video of snow falling on bamboo. I was mesmerized for a good five minutes watching the snow pile up on the bamboo. It started to bend, and not just a little bit. It was in a full forward fold, somehow holding the weight of the snow. I honestly thought it would crack under pressure. I kept waiting for the breaking point, but as the snow piled up and got heavier and heavier, it reached a stage where the thick white snow gently slid off the bamboo, and the beautiful jade plant gracefully resumed its standing position seemingly unshaken.

That is great for bamboo, but how the heck do we do that as humans? How do we let something heavy and unexpected, like snow in the temperate climate bamboo grows in, slide off us with ease and elegance?

For insight, I often turn to my yoga teachers and the timeless Yoga Sutras. I have studied with my teacher for over nine years, most recently in completing a 1,000-hour yoga therapy program. My teachers had to pivot halfway through the program due to Covid. I had the privilege to observe them truly embody the practices they taught. When at one point something difficult and seemingly gut-wrenching happened to them, on top of having to change their delivery methods and have their studio close due to Covid, they didn't snap under the pressure; instead, they taught us the concept of ishvara pranidhana.

Ishvara pranidhana is the practice of fully surrendering to the Highest or Source or the "Great Manitou," as my grandfather used to say. According to the Yoga Sutras, "In surrendering the ego to the Supreme Being in humility, it is thought that the character of the Divine can be attained."

My teachers taught that surrender is the ultimate yogic practice when you encounter a situation that rocks your foundation or pushes you past your limits. It is one that if truly done, brings great peace of mind. I learned when you can surrender or give up control (that you don't actually have anyway) without being a victim to the circumstance, something magical happens. Usually, things turn out better than expected. It requires faith in something bigger than us or this 3D reality. It is also very contrary to our mind and basic instincts. Our mind tries to control everything to keep us safe. Our minds push against, try to figure out, obsessively ruminate, and strategize.

Surrender is the opposite. It is a profound giving up of strategizing, controlling, or fighting against a difficult situation. We don't give up, rather we give it to a Higher Power and let go. It also entails a surrender to the present moment or the "power of now" as Eckhart Tolle teaches. When I observe myself and my thoughts, I always notice that most of the weight (snow) I'm carrying is in my mind and may not have been true or real. When I surrender to the "now," I notice I am actually okay. It is at that moment that the snow starts to dissipate.

Circling back to what does being resilient look like, in addition to possessing shock absorbers and a fully charged battery, it is about taking a stance that is rooted and therefore not easily blown around in the wind. It is trusting in life and the present moment and always looking up to Source, just like the bamboo.

This leads us to the final point of the definition, the notion of bouncing back after some adverse event. **Research suggests that resilient people don't just bounce back, one could say they actually "bounce" forward.** They may transcend what happened in that they are past the adversity, but they almost always contain the experience. Most will have learned and grown from dealing with the unexpected circumstance and are stronger, and maybe even better, for it.

Covid is a vivid example because we can all relate. We cannot go back to what was before Covid. We are collectively conscious of that fact as we refer to a "new normal" as opposed to going back to what was. If we are aware and intentional about it, I would argue we have grown a lot. We had the opportunity to stare fear in the face and overcome it, to develop anxiety-easing coping skills, to choose inclusion over division, and to adopt love as our dominant stance. I hope we are all better, wiser, and more compassionate as a result. And that is what resilient people tend to embrace.

Although resilience is ultimately about personal strength, it is also about vulnerability and faith. When something unexpected and possibly adverse transpires, like those bumps in the road, we don't fight them. We take a breath, know our battery is charged and our shock absorbers are in place, and then radically accept the ride.

I love teaching the theory, and our participants enjoy the examples, but I always get asked, "How do we actually build the shock absorbers, charge our batteries, and become as elegant under pressure as a bamboo forest?" That is what this book is about.

We turn to the American Psychological Association (APA) to start us off. They state: "Resilience is NOT a trait that people either have or do not have. It involves behaviors, thoughts, and actions that can be learned and developed in anyone."

BOOM!

That statement is hugely insightful. Thank you, APA. I need to repeat it: **resilient individuals have behaviors, thoughts, and take actions that make them resilient.** It is not because they are lucky or born that way. It is because they have certain habits wired in their brains, from repeated daily practice, that make them resilient. It also means we can all cultivate our resilience and become stronger, happier, and healthier.

Resilience is not a characteristic gifted to some individuals and not others. It can be learned and developed. It is also not a passive quality, but an active process. A process we are now embarking on. Once I learned this important fact, I went on a journey to discover these habits, behaviors, thoughts, and actions. What I discovered about the habits and behaviors of these resilient individuals is often a disappointment to the analytical, critical mind. These habits and behaviors are not something out of a secret scroll. They are very basic, even common sense, but NOT common practice.

Even if you already know this information, the key is to ask yourself if you are actually doing these things.

So now close your eyes and bring to mind someone who you know to be a "grace under fire" kind of person. Can you identify any of their behaviors, habits, thoughts, and actions? When I do this exercise, I immediately imagine a great boss of mine. We worked closely together for years, and I was witness to her behaviors, not only on the good days but also on the tough ones. It amazed me to see her remain positive and calm under pressure. She also managed to be able to respond thoughtfully as opposed to with a knee-jerk reaction when someone took a jab at her or the organization. I learned quickly that she never started or ended her day without her mindfulness practices.

So, what did you come up with? The traits, behaviors, and actions generally observed by us in resilient people are not surprisingly supported by countless research studies and empirical evidence. They are also not random. In fact, the habits and behaviors can be categorized into three buckets. These resilient Jedis engage in practices that make them (i) physically strong, (ii) self-aware, and (iii) intentional.

Or as we like to say in our Resilient by Design programs, resilient individuals have sustained practices focused on three keystones for resilience:

1. **Physical mastery:** They sleep soundly, eat consciously, move often, and breathe slowly and smoothly.

2. **Self-awareness:** They are mindful, positive, recharged, and rested, and they connect authentically with others.

3. **Intentional orientation:** They have a clear sense of their values and purpose, create a vision, set congruent goals, and take mindful and deliberate action. They also have faith in something bigger than them and this seemingly concrete world we live in.

I have to admit that I did not engage in many, if not most, of these practices when I was operating with a low battery—and I suffered as a result. I thought I did not have enough time. What I realize now is that when we create these habits and wire them into our brain, we don't have to have more time. We can replace the habits we have now that are not serving us with those that do. And let's face it, no one has the time to go to hospitals for panic attacks or to miss days of work due to stress, back pain, etc.

Now it's time to Do the Work and BE Resilient

How well do you score on these traits? How resilient are you?

As a teenager, I always loved to complete the quizzes in *Cosmopolitan* magazine. Are you in love? How high is your self-esteem? Will you make good parents together?

Let's reflect, *Cosmo*-style. How resilient are you? Take five minutes and answer the questions in the following self-assessment.

Only you will see the results, so be honest with yourself. I encourage you to do the assessment again at the completion of the book, so you can compare with yourself. As Wayne Dyer said, "You don't need to be better than anyone else, you just need to be better than you used to be."

HOW RESILIENT ARE YOU?

Please reflect and rate yourself on a scale of 1–5

PHYSICAL MASTERY

1. I have low levels of energy and/or significant drops in energy during the day.

1   2   3   4   5

1 (Always low energy) 5 (Consistent high energy)

2. I limit my consumption of packaged or processed foods.

1   2   3   4   5

1 (I eat a lot of processed foods) 5 (I never eat processed food)

3. I exercise on a regular basis.

1   2   3   4   5

1 (I never exercise) 5 (I love to move my body often)

4. I sit for long periods of time without getting up to walk or stretch.

1   2   3   4   5

1 (Always) 5 (I rarely or almost never sit for long periods of time)

5. I walk for at least thirty minutes five or more days per week.

1   2   3   4   5

1 (I never walk; I prefer to drive) 5 (I never miss a day of walking)

6. I get at least seven hours of sleep at normal sleeping hours.

1   2   3   4   5

1 (I never get seven hours sleep)
5 (I love my sleep and get seven plus hours daily)

7. I often wake up feeling tired.

1   2   3   4   5

1 (I always wake up tired)
5 (I never wake up tired; I jump out of bed rested)

8. I know how to reset my central nervous system.

1   2   3   4   5

1 (No clue. What is my central nervous system?) 5 (Yes, when I notice I am getting stressed, I know exactly how to calm myself down)

TOTAL PHYSICAL MASTERY _____/ 40

SELF-AWARNESS

9. I tend to operate in crisis mode.

1   2   3   4   5

1 (Always in crisis) 5 (Rarely or never in crisis)

10. I find that small challenges at work or in life can unnecessarily set off my stress response.

1   2   3   4   5

1(Always) 5 (Never or rarely do small stressors impact me)

11. I have a meditation or mindfulness practice.

1   2   3   4   5

1 (Nope, no meditation or mindfulness in my life)
5 (I have a daily mindfulness practice)

12. I take time to express my appreciation for the people in my life and the blessings I enjoy.

1   2   3   4   5

1 (No, not really) 5 (I make a point to always express my appreciation for my many blessings)

13. I often sacrifice happiness in the moment to get my work done.

1   2   3   4   5

1 (Yes, I always sacrifice my happiness) 5 (I never sacrifice my happiness)

14. I have close personal relationships with people who I rely on for support in challenging times.

1   2   3   4   5

1 (I don't have close relationships) 5 (I do have close and solid personal relationships)

15. I regularly take work home on evenings and weekends.

1   2   3   4   5

1 (I always must take work home) 5 (Never, work stays at work. Homelife is sacred)

16. I take regular breaks during the day to renew and recharge.

1 2 3 4 5

1 (No, I don't take breaks; I power through) 5 (I always take breaks throughout the day)

TOTAL SELF-AWARENESS _____/ 40

INTENTIONAL ORIENTATION

17. I have a clear sense of meaning and purpose in my life..

1 2 3 4 5

1 (No, I don't) 5 (I do know my purpose)

18. I enjoy my work.

1 2 3 4 5

1 (Unfortunately, I hate my job) 5 (I do really enjoy my work)

19. I regularly make choices that are congruent with my values.

1 2 3 4 5

1 (No, I do not) 5 (I always make choices in line with my values)

20. I make an effort to spend time on self-reflection and personal planning.

1 2 3 4 5

1 (No, I don't have time for navel gazing)
5 (Self-reflection and planning is a priority)

21. I have a clear sense of my priorities.

1   2   3   4   5

1 (No, I am not sure what my priorities are)
5 (Yes, I am crystal clear on my priorities)

22. I have personal spiritual beliefs that give meaning to my life.

1   2   3   4   5

1 (I do not) 5 (I consider myself to be a highly spiritual person)

23. When a difficult situation arises, do I tend to feel like the victim or the owner?

1   2   3   4   5

1 (I am the victim; it happened to me)
5 (I am an owner of the situation; it happened for me))

24. I embrace silence in my life.

1   2   3   4   5

1 (My life is very loud; I am never alone)
5 (I make effort to be in silence daily)

TOTAL INTENTIONAL ORIENTATION _____/ 40

TOTAL OVERALL SCORE _____

If your over-all score was between:	Resilience rating	What this means for you
0–60	Resilience wake-up call	Your batteries need significant charging, and your resiliency shock absorbers are not in place. Please see this as a wake-up call to embracing more self-care and resilience-enhancing practices.
61–75	Low energy reserves	You have some resiliency-enhancing practices; however, if adversity strikes, you may not have the energy reserves to handle it with grace and ease. Please take this seriously.
76–91	Continue building your shock absorbers	You are taking care of yourself and have a reserve. Note, is there one resiliency keystone you need to work on, or do you have to get better across the board? Take the time to reflect and continue to build your resilience shock absorbers.
92–105	Resilient	Good for you! You engage in resilience-enhancing practices and seem to have the behaviors, habits, thoughts, and actions of resilient individuals. Don't stop here—let's go from good to great.
106–120	Resilient Jedi	Wow! Do you want a job coaching others to be resilient? Please consider it! Pat yourself on the back and keep up the good habits.

What do you need to work on most? What area did you score lowest in? Please note it and pay particular attention when reading that section.

PHYSICAL MASTERY   SCORE_____

SELF-AWARENESS   SCORE_____

INTENTIONAL ORIENTATION   SCORE_____

As we close this chapter, I would like you to imagine the possibility of being less stressed, healthier, more at ease, and more resilient. Do it now: close your eyes and imagine the highest version of yourself. I bet you are vibrantly healthy, strong, and at ease.

Hold that image and make it real. The goal is to step into that possibility. It is possible—and it is time.

Chapter 2

CRITICAL SUCCESS FACTORS ON YOUR JOURNEY TO RESILIENCE

Without practice, nothing can be achieved.
—YOGA SUTRA

I love—and have countless—self-help and personal development books. I have read many from front to back, but I've started and never finished probably 75 percent of them. They still line my bookshelf, making me look very deep and contemplative. Often, the titles alone send me a message. A good one I notice often is *Feel the Fear and Do It Anyway* by Susan Jeffers. I tell myself I didn't really need to read the whole book, as I got and continue to receive the key message.

But seriously, I do not think I am alone in buying books, programs, and gym memberships, and never using them, not starting, or not following through. I read that at a subconscious level, 99 percent of us are wired to avoid change, as it is perceived to our brains as dangerous. More on that in the chapter on neuroscience.

My hope here is not that you read the whole book—which I know sounds funny—rather my goal is that you implement even one or two of the practices for an extended period of time and see what happens.

Here are the four hacks to help you get through:

1. The first key is to accept that building resilience is not about knowing but doing, and it starts with creating a practice. The content is so simple, but the hardwiring in our brain is complex. Therefore, daily intentional practice is the secret to morphing ourselves into someone who is more resilient and happier.

A practice implies habitual action in an effort to master that action.

Think about learning to play an instrument. About half a year prior to Covid, I bought my husband, Aubrey, a guitar. Until the lockdowns started, he took a few lessons and would pick it up once in a while and play. Once we got locked down, there was nowhere to go and nothing to do. He started playing daily, following a simple guitar app. After dinner, he sat down with the guitar and practiced. Much to our surprise, his fingers started to glide naturally between notes. He was suddenly able to read the music, move his hands accordingly, and sing all at the same time. Through daily practice, he rewired his brain and became a new person—he became a guitar player.

Patañjali's Yoga Sutras, which were written somewhere around the first century, state: "Mere philosophy will not satisfy us. We cannot reach the goal by mere words alone. Without practice, nothing can be achieved."

One of the biggest lessons I learned is to stop edutainment. If we want to change, we have to just do it.

2. The second key is directly connected. It is taking deliberate action. All new practices require action and repetition. This is not just based on the 2,000-plus-year-old Yoga Sutra, but on cutting-edge research into the neuroscience of behavior change. To create new pathways in your brain, a new way to be, you need to continue repeating the new habit until it becomes entrenched.

Resilient individuals take action in furtherance of their goals.

To make this easier, this book and related programs offer information on what to do and the reasons for it, but the main purpose of each chapter is to set the stage for the challenge exercises, which are your personalized action plan.

These challenge exercises are your tools for getting into action, adopting new practices, and creating a new normal for yourself. In each challenge exercise, I ask that you identify one teeny-tiny action item and commit to it for a minimum of two weeks. While I hope that some of these practices become permanent, two weeks is the minimum period of time required to see benefits.

3. The third critical success factor is to create some form of accountability. I am very good at getting things done when I have an externally imposed deadline from a teacher, professor, or boss. But when I do not, no way. I procrastinate the heck out of everything I commit to, to the point of convincing myself it is not important or meant to be, and sometimes, I'll drop it all together. It seems that I am "an obliger," to use Gretchen Rubin's phrase. In her book *The Four Tendencies* she covers the four archetypes and how they meet expectations. There are upholders who meet all expectations both internal and external; questioners who meet internal expectations but not external; rebels who resist all expectations; and finally, obligers who meet external expectations but not internal ones. Rubin suggests that the majority of us tend to fall into that last category. The reality for most of us obligers is that we will do things for other people but not for ourselves.

Rubin writes, "Obligers meet deadlines and follow through for bosses, colleagues, spouses, and so on—but don't follow through on things they want to do for themselves. If there are no external expectations, obligers almost always fail to complete the task, no matter how important it is to them."

I must admit, that's me. And it's why accountability is so important when creating and sticking to the practices of resilient individuals.

4. The final key to success in this program is to know your WHY. Your WHY should be emotional. It cannot be: "I want to build resilience to be stronger." Or "I want to do this to get healthier."

I worked with a client once who kept saying she wanted to get healthier, but she kept sabotaging herself. It was frustrating because we would meet week after week, and she didn't implement any of the practices she wanted to. I really felt like I was failing her. One day, exasperated, I asked her, "Do you really want to be healthy?" She was very unwell, and her doctors made some specific lifestyle recommendations for her to follow that she was not following.

Without hesitation she said, "Yes, of course, I want to be healthy."

I then asked, "Why? Why do you want to be healthy?"

"I want to be healthy so I can have my life back and be normal and have energy."

"Okay, great, but why do you want to have your life back and be normal and have energy?"

And for every answer, I followed up like a curious little child with "Why?"

Suddenly she went silent and then began to cry. "I am scared of dying and leaving my kids. I don't want them to be orphans or to have to bury their mother."

She was sobbing so badly. But that was the raw, deep, and powerful WHY that became her guiding light. We both wrote it down, and she placed it by her bedside, in her kitchen, on her phone, and everywhere around her house to remind her to get into action doing the things that would bring her body into equilibrium. And guess what? This WHY motivated the sh*t out of her. When it was hard to make change, she thought of her kids. She stopped self-sabotaging and realized that doing things to care for herself was actually caring for the well-being of her kids.

Keep asking yourself "why?" Why do you want this? Why? Why? Why? Sabrina, the publisher of this book, eloquently told me that "Your why should make you cry!"

Clearly, it works. **If your WHY makes you cry, it will give you the motivation to stick it out when sticking to your new behaviors is hard and feels uncomfortable.** Have your WHY written out. Write it out on stickies and place it all over your home and office to keep it top of mind.

Now it's time to Do the Work and BE Resilient

Complete the following Know Your WHY exercise. When you understand why you want to do or achieve something, you are more likely to see it through. This book will ask for some effort. The exercises and challenges will require you to take action over a period of time, and in some cases even ask you to change your routines.

For this reason, the very first exercise we ask of our participants is to outline their **WHY**.

1. Think of someone you consider to be resilient, a real grace-under-fire kind of person you admire. How do you perceive their energy and vitality?

   ....

   ....

   ....

   ....

2. If you had enhanced resilience, how do you think you would show up in the world? Consider a more resilient you with coworkers, your boss, and your spouse and kids. How does that make you *feel?*

   ....

   ....

   ....

   ....

3. WHY? WHY? WHY? Why would you like to be more resilient? Dig deeply. Recall your WHY should make you cry.

....

....

....

....

4. Now create your **WHY Power Statement**. Distill down into one sentence how will you benefit from enhanced resilience.

....

....

....

....

Consider also hiring a coach. If you are looking for a coach, we have a whole network of Certified Resilience Coaches who have completed our program. Send us an email at welcome@leadershipwellness.ca.

Chapter 3

THE OVERWHELM AUDIT

Simplify. Simplify. Simplify.
—Henry David Thoreau

Overwhelm seems to be a sign of the times these days. I hear it and see it everywhere. It's not just that we have too many competing responsibilities and are on all the time, we are also bombarded with data. Neurologist Dr. Richard E. Cytowic teaches that the human brain operates at very low speeds of about 120 bits (~15 bytes) per second. By comparison, the average internet provider shoots 75 megabytes of data per second into our homes, which is 5,000 times the rate that our brains can handle. Just that knowledge alone shows why most of us frequently feel overwhelmed: the sheer speed of our life, the gargantuan volume of data, the competing priorities, and 24/7 communication is simply too much.

And yet we continue—overextended, overcommitted, and overwhelmed.

In our Certified Resilience Coach Program, we teach our participants, all executive coaches and senior-level people managers, that we cannot start coaching someone to become more resilient when they are spinning out of control.

Recall my fall. At that moment when I was basically operating in crisis mode most of the time, I could not start implementing new resilience-enhancing habits and behaviors. That would have simply tipped me over the edge. You must assess and address the overwhelm first.

Let's assess first. Fill out the overwhelm audit on the next page.

Prior to doing this work, I scored almost all right-side answers, as I am sure many of you do as well. The right side indicates you are scattered, you have a limited sense of your priorities, and you have no practices to support the management of your overwhelm.

OVERWHELM AUDIT

Dealing with Overwhelm

Enhancement

	Less O/W	More O/W
Do you have a sense of your priorities?	Y	N
Are you a perfectionist?	N	Y
Have you set personal boundaries for time and space?	Y	N
Do you tend to think about too many things at the same time?	N	Y
Do you find yourself scattered, jumping from one thing to the next?	N	Y
Do you take on too much, have too many responsibilities?	N	Y
Do you have a hard time saying **no** to people's requests?	N	Y
Do you have a hard time delegating tasks to others?	N	Y
TOTAL		

The ability to manage overwhelm is key for working through unexpected challenges and becoming more resilient. And it is important to note that it is not about working faster and harder. Learning to deal with overwhelm is more than just trying to juggle a million things at once. In fact, it is the opposite.

So, what does dealing with overwhelm really boil down to?

Eradicating overwhelm entails narrowing your perspective on what really matters, being strategic, and getting into action.

The following three keys to diminishing overwhelm are habits or best practices that helped me (and now countless others) to get a grip on my scattered brain and life:

KEY 1: Take back your morning.

The first key is to take back your morning. I used to get up, always later than I had planned, and race around, get the kids off to school, run to work, then jump on the computer or into a series of back-to-back meetings. Although I knew better from all my pretty self-help books, I did not spend a moment considering how I wanted my day to go or what I really needed to be done prior to getting into email.

"Email is a receptacle filled with other people's requests on our time." I heard Brendan Bouchard say that on a podcast and it really, really resonated. I used to get to work and open up my email and boom, within seconds, my day was hijacked as I got sucked into other people's requests, issues, and needs.

If you are starting off your day with other people's priorities, you are being diverted from your goals and objectives right from the outset.

Owning your morning is both a philosophy and a practice. It says, "I am going to start my day in a particular way. I will take a bit of time for self-care, and I will establish how I want the day to go, how I want to show up, and what I want to accomplish." And most importantly, it says, "I will do all of this before engaging with the world, its energies, expectations, and priorities."

How do you own your morning? By creating and committing to a morning ritual that serves YOU. For me personally, I cannot go downstairs, or I will start cleaning and preparing food, not to mention if my kids see me, it's over. Instead, I sneak to the bathroom, brush my teeth, and scrape my tongue (an Ayurvedic best practice). I return to my bedroom and hopefully my husband is off doing his thing downstairs. I then do my yoga, pranayama (breathing exercises), and short meditation.

After my yoga practice, I used to think about the things I wanted to get done during the day. Now I do this the night before. It clears my head before sleep and sets me up for the morning routine. Specifically, I think about how I want to show up and feel the next day as well as the things I want/need to get done. I make a list, and normally I limit it to three things. There is a book by Gary Keller I recommend called *The One Thing*. Actually, this is one of those books where the title says it all! What I like about this book is that Keller has identified that behind every successful person is their ONE thing. Only the ability to dismiss distractions and concentrate on their ONE thing creates extraordinary results.

Imagine if you could get ONE thing done each day that was important to your long-term goals. How far ahead would you be on your life path after a month? Where would you be after a year? I put this book down as my ONE thing for half a year and despite the fact that I still had to run my business, finish my yoga therapist training program, and be a mommy (read: feed the family, clean the house, meal plan and grocery shop, help with homework, make schedules, and get to activities on time, not to mention dentist and doctor appointments), I did it! I prioritized this book and did my ONE thing.

As part of that I like to think about the "not-to-do items." What can you not do? What is not a priority right now? What can you delegate, postpone, or say "no thank you" to? This is hard for me, as I HATE saying no to people. I am a people pleaser and want to say yes. I want to help and frankly, to be liked. I am also easily distracted and sucked into other projects and issues that are sparkly. I am really working on strengthening the focus neuropathway in my brain. But I do know that getting the not-to-do items off the table will help you focus on getting ONE or two things done that are important.

And that is a great segue into the second key to dealing with overwhelm: becoming more efficient.

KEY 2: Become more efficient.

The original expression I toyed with using here was *become more productive*, but the word "productive" is so overused, and it carries, for me anyway, an energy of doing more with less. The actual definition of the word productive is *capable of producing a desired result*. I like that. So how do we become capable of producing a desired result calmly and in so doing, reduce our stress levels? **It's all about doing less.** Yay!

The first behavior is to stop multitasking. Many of us have heard that there is really no such thing as multitasking. When you multitask, what you are really doing is continuously starting and stopping progress on multiple projects in parallel. This is not an efficient way to get things done, and it actually limits our ability to focus. Becoming highly efficient involves uni-tasking. Do one thing. There is it again: *ONE thing*. Finish your one thing, or just complete it for the day, then do the next thing. Sabrina, my publisher, introduced me to the Pomodoro Technique whereby you set your timer for twenty-five minutes and do only that one thing. After the timer goes off, you have a five-minute break to meditate, stretch, or run to the loo. Then you reset your timer for another twenty-five minutes and can focus on another ONE thing.

The second behavior to becoming more efficient and, therefore, helping to ease your overwhelm is doing a brain dump to get your to-do list out of your head. The to-do list has a lot of benefits. It allows you to see all the things you want to do, prioritize them, and eliminate what is not important or strategic. Then get into action, one item at a time. There is a really good reason to get that list down on paper. It has also been proven that writing down your list serves to get all those items out of your head where they can distract you from being present and productive.

Another trick to efficiency is to tap into your productivity rhythms. Some of us are morning people, and others are best in the evenings. Knowing when your brain fires fastest is important for planning your day. Don't fight your productivity rhythms. Schedule your important and high-focus items for the correct part of your day and the easy, mechanical stuff for when your brain is in recovery. My husband and I are opposites. I am not able to really focus or be productive until at least 10 a.m. He can jump into work at 7 a.m. If I start at that hour, I just hate it and will look for ways to distract myself. My peak work times, when I'm most productive, are from 10 a.m. to 4 p.m., or maybe even 11 a.m. to 4 p.m., if I am honest. I can also easily work in the evenings or on the weekends, but don't take my morning ease time away from me!

Finally, eliminate distractions. TV, internet, and social media kill your efficiency. We know this. It's common sense but not common practice to shut off our phones and various notifications with their fancy rings. In fact, my phone just beeped with a text, and I'm exercising ALL MY WILLPOWER to not look at it. I forgot to put it in silent mode. Dang! Turn off anything that will beep, ring, buzz, or flash onto your screen while you are working, and your productivity will jump! I also put on some productivity/focus binaural beat music and set a time for myself, usually not longer than forty-five minutes. Knowing I have a time limit actually helps me to focus, and as my mind wanders, I bring it back mindfully over and over again.

KEY 3: Protect yourself.

The third key to dealing with overwhelm is to protect yourself. We have a funny expression in Polish: "trzymaj się," which directly translates to mean "hold yourself." No one will protect you and hold you but you. It helped me to start visualizing holding myself as a child. Maybe because I am a mom, I could resonate with protecting the child version of myself and really loving how silly and joyful she was.

What does protect yourself really mean? I did not protect myself that day I fell back on my head. I put everyone and everything ahead of what I wanted and needed to get done. I was frazzled and not even thinking rationally. I love my kids so much, but a good lesson for them would have been that sometimes they need to play alone. I also could have canceled the call with a colleague and considered making a simple dinner instead of a feast while feeling strapped. I could have taken time to breathe or to lie on the grass, which always recalibrates me. But I didn't protect myself—I threw myself into busyness and paid the price for many years to come.

Along with the stance to protect yourself, other things to consider doing include staying present. If I had taken a moment to get present that day, I would have noticed I was stressed. When stressed, we don't think straight, and therefore, make poor decisions with our reptilian brain. I could have taken a few breaths, brought my rational brain online, and probably would have made the decision to stop, drop (all my to-dos), and chill.

Staying present to what you are doing is the only way to get it done. Eckhart Tolle teaches us this so well in *The Power of Now*. "Now" is all there really is. In yoga, we learn that focusing on the future just gives us anxiety, and ruminating on the past, depression. Plus, if your mind is not focused on the actions required in your present task, then it is worrying about what you did or didn't do yesterday or what you have to do tomorrow. **Dwelling on regret or fear of failure is a great way to get totally stuck in overwhelm.** If you find your mind wandering, take a two-minute breathing break and bring your focus back to the task at hand. Again, I like to set a specific time to stay focused, even ten minutes is a good start. Check out the

Pomodoro Method. I'm using it as I write. Set a timer and focus, bringing your mind back every time you feel it wandering from the task at hand. We will do a much deeper dive on these practices in Module 2 when we discuss mindfulness.

Take regular breaks

Taking breaks may seem obvious, but it's a great tool for being efficient and productive. Get up walk around, jump up and down after your focus timer goes off. Changing your focus after a period of concentration is actually critical to staying focused and in action. Did you know even a thirty-second microbreak can increase your productivity up to 13 percent? Or that a fifteen second break from staring at your computer screen every ten minutes can reduce your fatigue by 50 percent? This data was found on LifeHack.com, but a Google search on the importance of work breaks will show lots of similar results.

Keep your state high. Tony Robbins talks a lot about this concept; he calls it the peak state. I didn't notice before if I was hungry until I was starving, same with thirst or going to sleep. Again, it is common sense that if we are exhausted, we are more likely to feel overwhelmed. We simply don't have the energy to handle all our tasks. If you're hungry, exhausted, or utterly deprived of fun, your willpower will collapse as well. I wish I had known all this in university. I remember sitting at my desk as a grad student at 3 a.m., so tired my eyes were falling with heaviness. I wasn't productive or efficient. I have no idea how I did as well as I did. It must have been the sheer power of youth and some kind of knowing I would get through it. It is no coincidence, though, that I used to get sick a lot. Especially after the exam crunch.

Keep your state physically high by ensuring you take consistently good care of yourself. In fact, this is what the first module of the program is about—sleeping well, eating right, and exercising.

It is also about keeping your mental/emotional state high. Consider the signs and vibes that a motivated person radiates. They smile, they laugh, and they more often than not shine with optimism. It's true that certain experiences cause these reactions, but this is only half the truth. Being happy, open to change, and optimistic also work the other way—you choose these feelings first, making you predisposed to positively evaluating the task at hand, your life, and what the future brings if you accomplish your objectives.

We will dive into this awesome material in Section 3 when we talk about generating positivity.

For now, find joy and have fun. Seriously, plan fun stuff and time with friends when you can laugh and relax. Think about what brings you joy and lean into it. **It's hard to feel overwhelmed when you are joyful.**

And finally . . . simplify. Life never needs to be as complicated as we make it.

Now it's time to Do the Work and BE Resilient

Review the overwhelm audit. Make note of how many over-whelm-causing behaviors you demonstrate and consider strategies for eliminating overwhelm.

Finally, take a moment to complete the first challenge exercise:

OWN YOUR MORNING

For the duration of the book (and beyond) start your day with a bit of self-care and intentionality. Specifically, determine what is most important for that day. The instructions are simple. Prior to doing anything else, especially checking email/text/social media, do the following things:

1. Wake up fifteen minutes earlier than you normally do.

2. Stretch and drink some water.

3. Write an intention for the day: ONE THING to accomplish and/or one feeling to generate.

4. Identify priorities and think about how you want to show up in the world today.

Chapter 4

NEUROSCIENCE IS YOUR BEST FRIEND

Progress is impossible without change,
and those who cannot change their minds cannot change anything.
—George Bernard Shaw

As I wrote the title for this section, I felt a slight tightening in my gut—what if I lose you here at this spot? Neuroscience, although more mainstream, still sounds foreboding. Strangely, this is my favorite lesson to teach in our Certified Resilience Coach Program and brings the most "ahas," not only to the participants, but strangely, to me each time I teach it.

Why neuroscience here and now as we embark on building resilience?

Ever since I was a teenager, I was a self-help book junkie. Even as a university student, I remember choosing to buy a self-help or spiritually oriented book over a dinner out. Books such as *The 7 Habits of Highly Effective People*, *Think and Grow Rich*, *The Power of Positive Thinking*, and *Heal Your Life* lined my bookshelf. I had and read so many of these books, but I could only implement the best practices I learned for a few days to, at best, two weeks. I could meet school and work deadlines and deliverables; but without some external accountability, I could not wake up at 5 a.m. like I continually promised myself after reading the *The 5 AM Club*, or go to the gym, meditate daily, stop eating sugar, or countless other goals I set for myself. This made no sense to me, and I was often disappointed in myself. "Why am I not doing the things I 'should' and actually want to do?" I would ask myself.

More frighteningly, why, even with a concussion, did I attempt to run around, serve, and worry about others? I knew I should go and rest in a quiet dark room, but I was determined to make dinners from scratch, take on big work projects, and vacuum the house despite knowing that I was jeopardizing my healing. Was I nuts? My husband thought so. What I now know is that **I was operating on autopilot habits that were wired in my limbic brain**.

Here's the value of diving into neuroscience—it naturally sets us up for success in implementing the habits and behaviors of resilient individuals. There is little point learning about the habits if we are not going to actually apply them consistently. The latest research shows when it comes to changing your behavior, you'll have more success if you use and put your brain to work for you.

CHANGE

We hear the only constant in life is change and that the measure of intelligence is the ability to adapt. But the problem is most of us are resistant to change, and not just a little resistant but a lot. If you don't agree, consider this: Even when faced with a life-threatening situation, people tend to resist change despite knowing the repercussions. Here is a shocking example described by Dr. Edward Miller from Johns Hopkins University. Dr. Miller talks about heart disease patients who have undergone bypass surgery. Their underlying condition is generally caused by lifestyle choices, and the bypass surgery only briefly alleviates chest pains but does not prevent future heart attacks. The best way to correct this condition is through heart-healthy life-style change: basic stuff like walking and eating unprocessed foods and lots of fruits and vegetables. And yet despite knowing the grave consequences of not changing their lifestyle, two years after surgery, 90 percent of patients did not change their habits and behaviors. So here is a group of people who have already had heart surgery, told to change their lives or more complications will ensue, and 90 percent of them don't embrace the change. Do they not want to live? Dr. Miller said these results are quite typical. But why?

Why do we find it so hard to change, even when we know it's good for us?

The simple answer is that our brains are wired to love the familiar, stable, and secure. They are hardwired to protect us. I love how Dr. Rick Hanson, a psychologist, mindfulness teacher, and author teaches that the brain has a negativity bias. He says **the human mind "is like Velcro for negative experiences, but Teflon for the positive ones."**

In essence, the brain's tendency is to absorb and easily remember negative experiences as well as potential threats. That is then combined with its tendency to not so readily absorb and remember positive experiences. Dr. Hanson even shares that researchers have found that animals, including humans, generally learn faster from pain than pleasure. Sad, isn't it?

But it is part of our animal survival instinct. This Velcro/Teflon tendency of our brain is not our fault. It is there to protect us. The good news is we can counteract these negative bias tendencies deliberately, and by doing so, we can actually change our brains and ultimately change ourselves using our knowledge of neuroscience.

Let's back up a bit and define neuroscience.

Neuroscience is the study of the nervous system and brain. Like many, I thought that neuroscience was limited to the brain, but no. Because the nervous system sends signals from the spinal cord and the brain through the body and then back from all the body parts to the brain, it is a whole body experience. This ties beautifully into yoga, by the way.

The nervous system controls everything we do: breathing, walking, thinking, and feeling. This system is made up of our brain, spinal cord, and all the nerves of our body. The brain is the control center, and the spinal cord is like a major superhighway to and from the brain. The nerves carry the messages to and from the body, so the brain can interpret them and take action.

Nervous systems know-how:

- Central nervous system is the most crucial part of a living organism and is often called the central processing unit of the body. It consists of the brain, brainstem, and spinal cord.

- Peripheral nervous system, or the nerves outside the brain, connects the central nervous system to the limbs and organs.

- Autonomic nervous system is part of the peripheral nervous system that controls system functioning, such as digestion, heart rate, respiration, and perspiration.

- The sympathetic and the parasympathetic nervous systems are both components of the autonomic nervous system. These are very important to understand.

- The sympathetic nervous system is the stress response. It controls the body's response to perceived threat. "Perceived" being the key word here. It triggers a number of physiological changes that prepare the body to "fight or flight" by directing energy toward functions that are essential for survival. For example, adrenaline is released, heart rate speeds up, muscles contract, pupils dilate, digestion and urination are inhibited. Essentially, it prepares your body to run from danger.

- The parasympathetic system is the opposite. It controls the "rest and digest" functions of the body. It relaxes your body after a period of stress or danger. It also helps keep the basic functions of your body, such as digestion, running during times you feel safe.

While healing from my concussion, I learned from my functional neurologist that people who have a traumatic brain injury are basically operating in their sympathetic nervous system most of the time. In other words, they are in chronic states of fight or flight. I know this personally; for no apparent reason, my hands would shake. I shared with you that I couldn't sleep, I was easily overstimulated, and that small things, even if positive, were huge stressors. In a word, I felt shaken, which I guess my brain was, and I had to heal. I needed to do everything to still my body by tapping into my parasympathetic or "rest, digest, and heal system." This, along with yoga, is where I discovered the power of the vagus nerve, as my sessions with my neurologist were partially dedicated to stimulating this amazing wandering nerve (vagus literally means wandering, as this nerve seems to touch every organ and critical part of the body). His nurses had vagus nerve stimulators that they would use on my tongue, behind my ear, on certain parts of my face, and I would feel an immediate relief. I would honestly sigh and see my pulse rate go down on the finger pulse oximeter. I would also sleep better on those nights and not feel so shaken. They had their patients do this at least two times per week to start building the neural pathways associated with being calm.

As I dug into this further and with my yoga work, I started to see that this process applied not just to concussion patients but to everyone who is stressed, anxious, and overwhelmed. If your central nervous system is out of whack for whatever reason, your ability to activate the rest-digest-detoxify-heal part of the nervous system is significantly decreased. Over time, this leads to chronic inflammation and poor gut function, and consequently, can result in pretty much any chronic disease, including autoimmunity and cancer.

Of course, a dysregulated and unhappy central nervous system impacts the brain itself. So that brings us back to the gray matter at hand. Here is a diagram we use with the coaches we train:

THE THREE BRAINS

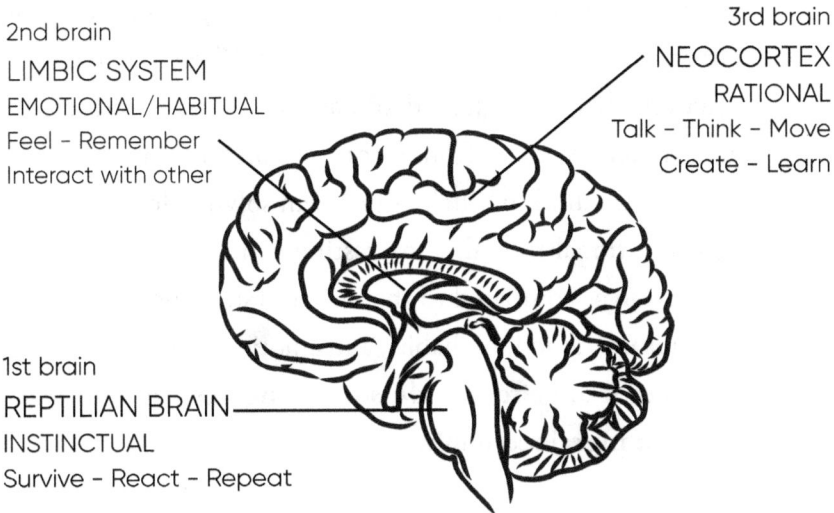

2nd brain
LIMBIC SYSTEM
EMOTIONAL/HABITUAL
Feel – Remember
Interact with other

3rd brain
NEOCORTEX
RATIONAL
Talk – Think – Move
Create – Learn

1st brain
REPTILIAN BRAIN
INSTINCTUAL
Survive – React – Repeat

Although considered simplistic by some, the triune brain analogy is the best way to explain how our brains operate.

The triune brain has three parts:

1. The reptilian brain, which is responsible for our primary drivers such as eating, sleeping, and sex. This part of our brain is instinctual and primarily focused on survival.

2. The limbic system is where memories are formed and habits learned. It is also the center of our emotional experiences and our connection to other people. The limbic system is the home of the amygdala, the superhero that wants to protect us from danger and can quickly put us into fight, flight, or freeze.

    What is interesting to note is that habits live in an area of the brain that is more or less automatic. In other words, when cued, habits can be triggered automatically. For example, starting my car triggers the habit of adjusting the seat, putting on my seat belt, changing the radio station, looking in my rearview mirror, then backing out of my driveway. There is a sequence of actions that are ingrained and automatic when triggered.

3. Finally, there is the prefrontal cortex, which is responsible for higher order thinking such as problem solving, logic, creativity, and rational thought. Interestingly, it takes more energy to function as compared to the limbic system, which governs those automatic actions, habits, and emotion. What that means is **it takes more effort to do something new than to react out of an ingrained habit.**

Dr. Dan Siegel, a neuropsychiatrist, uses the hand as a model of the brain to explain how the various parts of the brain work together, with the fingers, palm, and wrist each representing a different section. What is neat about his "Hand Model of the Brain" is that when we make a fist and turn our hand toward us, our hand actually looks like a mini brain. He explains by using a fist how one section of the brain, specifically the prefrontal cortex responsible for higher order thinking, can be cut off from the other parts of the brain during times of stress, causing us to "flip our lid." When we flip our lid our lower brain takes over—we are then driven by habits, emotions, and survival instinct.

I first saw Dr. Siegel (whose book *Whole-Brain Child* I read repeatedly to figure out why my kids were having regular tantrums and meltdowns) present this concept. He used the hand model of the brain to explain to small children what happens when they get upset, stressed, or have a complete "lying on the ground in the store screaming" kind of breakdown. It made so much sense, and I realized, just like he did, that it doesn't just apply to children.

We can now make the link to resilience. When an adverse, unexpected event occurs in our day, if our amygdala is highly reactive, we will lose connection with our higher order thinking upstairs brain and react with our downstairs emotional, habit-driven survival instincts.

BOOM!

Now imagine if you are a leader of an organization, a teacher, a doctor, or a lawyer, and you are subject to multiple stressors a day. You actually lose your capacity to think and make decisions for your company, team, and people, not to mention yourself!

The other point here is to note that as we embark on building resilience-enhancing habits, we must be aware of this brain model to keep our prefrontal cortex in place to, for lack of a better expression, keep our old habits in check and intentionally instill new ones with less of a struggle.

A WORD ON HABITS

As we know, much of what we do daily is habitual—we do these things without appearing to think about it: driving a car, brushing our teeth, browsing social media, or putting on our pants.

Habits, rituals, and routines as we now know are formed in the basal ganglia, which is part of our limbic structure and can be performed efficiently and without much effort.

Changing a habit or embedding a new behavior, on the other hand, fires up our prefrontal cortex. Doing so requires effort and focused attention. Overriding ingrained habits can feel physically uncomfortable and even painful.

I recall trying to quit drinking coffee that, for the record, I used to LOVE. My doctor said I had to quit this joyful, daily practice as I had post-concussion syndrome insomnia. Logically, coffee or any caffeine is not a good idea when your body is in a constant state of fight or flight and is not sleeping. I also have now learned that coffee is really an enemy if you are stressed or anxious.

Caffeine is the most widely consumed central nervous system stimulant. It stimulates brain cells, called neurons, and their activity in the brain. What that means is each time you sip that latte, your neurons fire. Your pituitary gland senses this firing and thinks it is an emergency, so it alerts your adrenals to pump out adrenaline and cortisol. In short, caffeine instantly puts you into fight or flight mode. It can flip your lid! If you're drinking several cups a day, it's likely your whole nervous system is on constant alert without you even knowing it.

Please consider ditching this habit or at least crowding it out, especially if you suffer from stress or anxiety. I first decreased the volume, then I switched to Swiss water decaf (lots of coffee is decaffeinated using toxic chemicals), and then I was simply able to skip it. I felt a strange sort of freedom when that happened; when I no longer felt headachy or tired when I did not have my "hit" of coffee. I use the word "hit" intentionally. As it turns out, caffeine is a psychoactive drug. Now I only occasionally have a decaf when it is an event at a nice café with good friends.

At the time the neurologist cut me off, though, coffee was not only an addiction, but a deeply embedded, encoded event in my life associated with many positive emotions and feelings. I literally felt lost, like I didn't know what to do with myself when the time came to have my morning coffee. Herbal tea or warm water with lemon just did NOT do it for me. I had to override that deeply engraved neural pathway using my prefrontal cortex, and it felt awful. I was not happy, and I swore at my doctor. I thought it was stupid all because my brain was wired this way. I had to use my prefrontal cortex to override this habit that I started at age sixteen. I used a powerful, emotional WHY statement, and I literally pasted it over my beautiful stainless steel Jura espresso coffee machine that seemed to be waving me over. I also had accountability from my doctor, not to mention my husband who was invested in me starting to sleep again.

And I did it. Slowly, I crowded out the coffee. But I must share that when that sticky paper would fall off the coffee maker, or when under pressure, tired, or distracted, my prefrontal cortex would lose focus, and I would relapse until a new neural pathway of a new morning routine was formed and embedded in my limbic brain.

SO HOW DO WE FORM NEW NEURAL PATHWAYS?

First, our brains are made up of billions of neurons that connect to one another through trillions of synapses or pathways that relay information. Neural pathways are created in the brain based on our actions and thoughts, like roads or paths in the brain. As an action or thought pattern is repeated, the road gets smoother and faster until a habit is created.

When I teach this, I always use the example of bushwhacking with my friend Danusia. I have accompanied her to her family's remote, rustic, heavenly cottage since I was seven years old. Her family owns 100 acres of land on a private lake. Although we could hike up and down the well-worn 3 km drive to the road, that was not as much fun as hiking up through the forest to go to a mountain-top look-out. At the beginning of the season when we would hike, there was literally no path. We would hike up in the general direction, and it was not easy. We would always return scratched up from all the bushes. Inevitably, there would also be fallen logs in the way that we would need to move, and it would take us a long time. Often, we would feel lost. As the season continued and we did the same walk over and over, a path was forged. We could see it, walk it quickly, and there was no guessing of the route.

It is the same with the neural pathways in the brain.

Psychologist Deann Ware explains that when brain cells communicate frequently, the connection between them strengthens and "the messages that travel the same pathway in the brain over and over begin to transmit faster and faster."

With enough repetition, these behaviors become automatic. Driving, riding a bicycle, even reading are examples of complicated activities that we do automatically and without thinking because neural pathways have formed.

So, the good news is we can use the understanding of how neural pathways are formed to our advantage when becoming more resilient, healthier, and happier. I remember hearing, even as a young adult, that "you can't teach an old dog new tricks," essentially that the brain was pretty much fixed and actually deteriorated after growth periods in childhood. Now, we know that's not true. **Your brain is capable of change until the day you die.** This is the process called neuroplasticity.

Neuroplasticity, also known as brain plasticity, is the ability of the brain to form new neural connections, grow new neural networks, and change its function and even physical structure as a result of learning, experiences, behaviors, memories, and thoughts.

Virtually everyone who studies the brain is astounded at how plastic it is.
–Kurt Fischer, Harvard Medical School

This was particularly interesting for me given my traumatic brain injury. Neuroplasticity meant I could heal and actually be better than before the injury by intentionally creating some new neural connections.

It turns out neuroplasticity works much like physical exercise does for the body—just as it takes time and repetition to build muscle, so does building neural pathways.

Reach now demonstrates that **consistently repeating an activity, behavior, feeling, or thought leads to physical changes in your brain.**

What's more, the process of neuroplasticity happens thousands of times a day, giving us vast opportunity to change ourselves if we put deliberate effort and commitment into making it happen. You can, therefore, change your behavior—even those difficult-to-break, ingrained habits—by being intentional and creating new neural pathways in your brain.

The obvious question for me was HOW? How do I use the plastic nature of the brain to heal and even more, transcend the habits that so often sabotage my dreams?

The practice of using your mind to assist in changing your behaviors and habits is called self-directed neuroplasticity.

Here is a four-step approach to use your mind to change your brain to create sustainable positive behavior change.

There are many versions of this approach. This is based on research and my own personal experience. When it seemed I could not heal from my concussion, I finally realized I had to rewire my brain. It had created new neural pathways and neural memories of pain, as well as insomnia, not to mention tinnitus. I also had to create new habits and behaviors in support of my healing, which were new and required habit change on my part.

STEP 1: Focus

The first step in building new neural pathways to create lasting positive habits is to focus your attention and take mindful action. Here is how we can do that:

- **Summon your thinking brain.** Recall the thinking brain / prefrontal cortex we talked about—we need to tap into it. When you first try to adopt a new behavior, you have to insert conscious, deliberate effort, intention, and thought into the process.

- **Pay attention.** Part of engaging our thinking brain is actively paying attention. This is mindfulness in action. When you stop paying attention because you're distracted or stressed, your brain reverts back to old patterns and ways of being. Paying attention means being really present with yourself and noticing your urges nonjudgmentally. Every time you perform the new behavior or override an impulse or craving, you make the old habit weaker in your brain.

- **Know your WHY.** Recall the emotional WHY that triggers our limbic brain and helps our prefrontal cortex override default patterns. Consciously think about how your life will improve by changing your behavior. Connect with your WHY and with the emotion associated with those reasons. Doing so will engage your limbic system, and your brain will start to give your willpower a helping hand.

- **Make your decision and take mindful action.** The more focused attention and mindful action we take, the more we will allow those neurons to connect. The more they connect, the more they wire together; and the more they wire together, the more they fire together. What that means is that they create new neural highways that fire automatically and manifest as a new behavior or a new state. In theory, this process is easy. But I struggled with it until I had a great WHY statement. I knew what I had to do. For example, in order to support my healing, I could not have any blue light at night or actually any stimulus. Gone was watching a movie with my family on a weekend or going out with friends in the evening. It seemed so boring to have to stay in, stay focused, and stay calm.

I think you have to start with the WHY. I wanted to heal. I wanted to sleep so that I could be present with my family, have fun, and also show up in my business as someone authentically well—mind, body, and soul.

I started to pay attention to my triggers; this was important. My cell phone was one of them. The text messages, social media scrolling (which I was sure I didn't do until I paid attention), and blue light were all stimuli. I, like most, was addicted to the dopamine hit of the cell phone—so I had to totally shut it off. It was so hard!

I felt disconnected. I made excuses such as I was just going to listen to (not watch) someone on YouTube while I cleaned the dishes, but then I would get sidetracked as I searched for what to listen to and would go down the rabbit hole of checking emails and texts and suddenly find myself sucked back into the social media vortex.

I made an intention, wrote out my WHY again, made a decision, and took mindful action.

STEP 2: Repeat often

I learned quickly that just because we have made a decision and perhaps even formed a new neural pathway, it does not mean that those habits will stick forever. Repetition is critical for lasting change. Once more! **Repetition is critical for lasting change.**

Recall the bushwhacking in the forest to create the path. We had to hike it many times over and over again for it to become a well-trodden, easy-to-follow path. I had to repeat my daily evening ritual of unplugging myself: no phone, no TV, no computer, no stimulus, no bright lights, no excitement.

As it turns out, as we create new neural pathways, the pathways get stronger with repetition until the behavior becomes our new normal. In terms of repetition, it is estimated that it takes 10,000 repetitions to master a skill and develop the associated neural pathway. Expect it to take between three and six months for a new behavior to become a habit, though this estimate varies by person, and I would argue, it depends on what the new habit is. For example, I do not think it would take several months to establish the highly pleasurable habit of eating dark chocolate after dinner. The timeframe is a gray area, as there are so many variables to consider.

What I do know is when the new behavior we want to establish as a habit isn't as pleasurable as eating bonbons, knowing it takes thousands of repetitions to establish helps us be more self-compassionate and keep going. Numerous times on my healing journey I would begin to feel better and would revert to the old behaviors because they were still etched in my brain, then bam, I was back at square one.

But knowing that I needed to keep up this new evening ritual for six months was a turning point. I kept reminding myself of the 10,000 hours to become an expert, only here it was 10,000 repetitions to heal.

STEP 3: Engage your senses and visualize success

Now we get to have fun! We have all heard of visualizing our way to success. Countless, if not most, self-help books refer to it, and many encourage using our imagination and creating vision boards to help draw what we want to attract into our life.

In yoga, we speak of a similar practice called "bhavana." In Sanskrit, bhavana refers to the notion of cultivating or bringing into existence. Yoga teaches that the power of the mind can be used to imagine not only feelings of compassion and kindness, but actual occurrences in one's life. For example, in my yoga therapy program, students were encouraged to visualize breathing in white healing light to the area of dis-ease. They were also encouraged to visualize themselves completely well and for us, the yoga therapists, to visualize them well. I found when I did this with my own students, strange occurrences would happen. Often the students would say things like, "You won't believe this, but what I was picturing actually happened . . ."

Why is this the case and how does this relate to the neuroscience of sustainable behavior change? We turn to one of my heroes, neuroscientist Dr. Joe Dispenza, who teaches that visualization can be a very powerful tool to build new neural pathways and therefore a new you.

Research shows having a vision and imagining yourself taking new action works because of how our brains are wired. We build neural pathways either through action in real life or visualizing that action. Did you catch that? We do not have to take actual action to create new neural pathways. We can, but we can also imagine taking the action and that builds a pathway as well.

For example, when we envision ourselves running up a staircase, the neurons in our brain interpret that imagined action (running up stairs) as having really happened. The neurons receive an impulse while we are visualizing that tells them to perform the movement. This then creates a new neural pathway and memory of how to do the action. You know you are doing it right when just by imagining something you get your heart racing, get goosebumps, or other physical sensation. Research studies have shown that groups who visualized the act of climbing stairs performed faster and improved their scores as compared to groups that did not visualize.

Dr. Dispenza explains that you make the neurological connections of your desired situation in the brain. Since our body cannot distinguish imagined from actual emotions, we can already experience the desired state. Dr. Dispenza calls this "mental rehearsal," where we mentally go through the same process over and over again. With the idea of "neurons that fire together, wire together," we build the neurological hardware in our brains for success.

"Over time you begin to map neurologically what your future will be like. If you do it enough times, it becomes a subconscious program. In other words, you're changing your body to be primed for a future subconsciously. When you do that enough times, that's when the synchronicities, the miracles, the coincidences, the opportunities will begin to show up in your life," he says.

Professional athletes utilize visioning to perfect their craft. Jack Nicklaus once said, "I never hit a shot, not even in practice, without having a very sharp, in-focus picture of it in my head . . . I 'see' the ball going there: its path, trajectory, and shape, even its behavior on landing." He used his brain to visualize his act so when he performed it in reality, his neurons were ready to perform.

Connecting a new behavior or habit you want to create to as many areas of the brain as possible helps to develop new neural pathways. Further, tapping into all five senses creates an anchor that helps the new neural pathways to stick. Consider connecting your successes at developing a new habit to as many senses as possible.

We all have experiences that have changed us. We can recall the sensations: the images, smells, how we felt, etc. You can do the same with your success at creating a new habit or new you.

What does your optimal health look like, what does it feel like, and what would you be doing if you had boundless energy? Imagine it, feel it, taste it—get goosebumps from it.

STEP 4: Accountability

The fourth and final step to creating sustainable behavior change is to build in some external accountability.

We already talked about this in the critical success factors. Having an accountability partner is HUGE. I am lost without it. Most of us are "obligers." Remember this term coined by Gretchen Rubin in her book *The Four Tendencies*? She found that the majority of us are obligers, so chances are, you're one as well. Call it ego, call it fear of looking bad, whatever it is, if we promise another we will do something, we are more likely to do it.

Also, having an accountability partner means that you will likely learn from the successes and failures of your partner, giving you access to their experiences and challenges. You'll learn how they overcame their hurdles. You can work with your accountability partner to brainstorm solutions to the challenges that are holding you back, and finally, you can celebrate your victories together.

Now it's time to Do the Work and BE Resilient

The work this week is simple. Focus on creating your accountability structure.

FIND AN ACCOUNTABILITY PARTNER

Choose your partner carefully. A good partner will be dedicated to this work and supportive of you both achieving better resilience. You want to find a partner who will support you and share a bit of their experience in reading the book with you. You can also recruit a friend to read the book with you. Consider meeting weekly for eight to ten weeks.

Objectives of first meeting with your accountability partner:

1. Share your WHY Power Statement and discuss its meaning with them.

2. Establish a weekly time and manner for a meeting. Discuss challenges you may face in committing to a weekly meeting and the best ways to overcome those challenges.

The last word on neuroscience:

Neuroscience is your best friend because you can tap into the power and function of your brain to create new neural pathways that result in a new, happier, healthier, more resilient you.

PART TWO.
KEYSTONES OF RESILIENCE

RESILIENCE KEYSTONE I:
PHYSICAL MASTERY

When health is absent, wisdom cannot reveal itself,
art cannot manifest, strength cannot fight, wealth becomes useless,
and intelligence cannot be applied.
−Herophilus

I had no idea how much our body mattered when it came to resilience or well-being. So much of my life I was stuck in my head, focused entirely on my mind to make me smarter, more productive, happier, and healthier. I knew eating and exercising were important, as we all do, but I had no idea they were the actual FOUNDATION to everything health and wealth until I bashed my head in.

Not everyone can relate to a traumatic brain injury, but just think back to a time you have had the flu or if you had Covid. When you are achy, exhausted, weak, and feel horrible, how can you possibly make good decisions, handle stress well, be creative, and show up as your best self? We all know you cannot. But similarly, you cannot be great when you are physically tired, your digestion is off, your immune system is sluggish or hyper reactive, your head hurts, or your back is achy. These are all common symptoms associated with stress, and many (if not most) of us in today's modern Western society are tolerating these symptoms or ignoring them and are just pushing through. Then if something unexpected happens, we fall apart because we do not have the reserves to handle it.

The body is the key! I learned this over and over again. Not only to listen to the body, but to treat it as our most prized possession.

I have a neighbor who has a high-performance Porsche. By all measure, this neighbor looks unhealthy. Eyes sunken, belly big, skin gray, but wow, does his car ever shine. Seems it is cleaned and polished daily. He gives more love to that car than his most important vehicle, his own body.

So, we start our resilience-enhancing journey by focusing on our physical well-being.

If you recall from the introduction, we discussed that resilient individuals have habits, behaviors, and take actions that make them physically strong. When we are physically well, we do more and show up better in the world, and we can also handle setbacks and adversity more gracefully. In a word, we can be more resilient.

We will cover four primary practices that build physical mastery:

1. **Sleep deeply.** We will explore the critical practice of sleeping soundly. We start with sleep because it impacts directly on just about every aspect of your body, health, energy, and productivity.

2. **Eat consciously.** We discover why eating consciously is imperative, not only to your resilience, but your overall health. We're going to explore the impact of the modern Western diet on your energy, productivity, and disease, and I will offer some guiding principles or strategies for how to nourish our bodies—including a Guide to Eating Consciously.

3. **Move often.** In this section, we discuss how to nudge ourselves to move often and make it a lifestyle, not just a thing to do three times a week.

4. **Breathe slowly.** Finally, we complete the Physical Mastery section by tapping into our hidden physical superpower: breath.

Remember to adopt one new habit at a time. The challenge exercises and bonus material provide numerous strategies for improvement. I want you to pick only one practice each week. Your one new practice should be one that provides impact for you AND is feasible for you to stick with, so choose carefully.

Also, stack your habits. What I mean by that is to pick one new habit each week and continue doing it as you add a new one the following week. One habit may not seem like a lot, but the real goal is to have ten new sustainable resilience-enhancing practices at the end of ten weeks.

You've got this!

Chapter 5

SLEEP DEEP

The advice I would give to my younger self is very, very simple:
Stop burning the candle at both ends and renew your estranged
relationship with sleep. You will be more productive, more effective,
more creative, and more likely to enjoy your life.

—Arianna Huffington

When I started teaching on the importance of sleep and sleep hygiene in our Resilient by Design program, I was actually a great sleeper. I could chuck myself into bed after a busy day anywhere, anytime. I could fall into a deep sleep after watching an intense movie, working on my computer, or scrolling through my phone. Of course, when I had my girls, I was very attuned to every sound that came from them. I would hear them cry "Mama" or even whisper it across the house, whereas my husband would need to be shaken awake. But aside from this maternal instinct, my sleep was "normal," and my issue was that I was simply not getting enough of it. I was going to bed way too late, often staying up working after the kids went to bed, and then waking up early to have my morning routine and a bit of "me time." On average, I was sleeping six to six and a half hours, but I was sleep deprived as my body needed more rest.

If you fall into this category, you are in luck because there is so much you can do to enhance your resilience just by making sleep a priority and implementing some sleep best practices.

I now realize there is another category of sleeper—those who struggle with insomnia. The Mayo Clinic defines insomnia as "a common sleep disorder that can make it hard to fall asleep, hard to stay asleep, or cause you to wake up too early and not be able to get back to sleep. You may still feel tired when you wake up. Insomnia can sap not only your energy level and mood but also your health, work performance, and quality of life." Yuperdoodles, as an old friend of mine used to say. That captures it.

I did not develop my insomnia right after my fall; it happened a little while later. I guess it happened when the injury settled in a bit. In fact, for the first while, I was sleeping a lot, and then the insomnia started and it was worse than any pain from the concussion. One night, I just could not settle. I tried to breathe and meditate, but nothing would help. I turned on a yoga nidra on my Insight Timer app. Usually I would not hear the end of it if I listened to one. Here I heard every single word. It was interesting to hear it all but so very frustrating at 2 a.m. I put on another yoga nidra. This time longer; thank God the app has several hundreds of them. Then I listened to another one. Again, I was awake for every word.

I was okay the next day. My head hurt more and my ears rang louder, but I was able to get through my daily work and mommy tasks. The next night, I collapsed into bed exhausted. I never anticipated a repeat of the sleepless yoga nidra night, but much to my dismay and disbelief, it happened again. Then again the night after that, and it kept up night after night. My life started to fall apart as did my body. My hands seemed to shake all the time, I dropped things, became forgetful and foggy. I developed diarrhea. My body was in total shock and sleep became a personal obsession. I took herbal pills, melatonin, did a slow yoga practice every night, dimmed the lights, drank warm milk with cinnamon, listen to binaural beats that would apparently lull me to sleep, sprayed the room with lavender, avoided all blue light, tried sleep hypnosis, did therapy, saw doctors, psychics, energy healers, and the list goes on. The concussion specialist said it was "normal" and prescribed antidepressants and very strong sleeping pills, whose list of side effects included "death." I politely declined, but the insomnia was relentless and truly like torture. I started to associate the bed with not sleeping but rather tossing and turning. Worse, since I was aware of the dangers of sleep deprivation, I became more anxious about sleep, and it became a self-reinforcing, self-fulfilling cycle of non-sleep.

If any of that resonates and you have a tendency toward insomnia, please skip past the section on the dangers of sleep deprivation. You do not need to know this! In fact, what helped me was unlearning some of it. A Cognitive Behavior Therapist (CBT) I worked with nudged me in this direction. In fact, he insisted that I note (and I had to write it in a daily diary) how high-functioning I was despite my lack of sleep. He also suggested that perhaps I did not need as much sleep as I thought I did. This helped me to relax about my non-sleep and to slowly break that anxiety about sleep causing more non-sleep cycles. I also reframed my insomnia from my greatest torture to my "great awakening." I told myself that this was time given to me to peacefully contemplate things that I could not otherwise. Maybe this was a gift and not just a test of my resilience to torture?

As I write this, I am still not back to 100 percent, and just like discussed earlier, being resilient doesn't mean, contrary to popular belief, that we just bounce back to what was prior to adversity. **Generally, if something big and difficult occurs in our life, we must grieve (pause), process (pause), and heal (pause), and then we can bounce forward "transcending and containing" our experience.** That was an expression one of my sociology professors at Queens University used to repeat. We must transcend but contain what happened so we can, in essence, become better than before the event.

So coming back to sleep wherever you may be on the spectrum of sleep, it is good to assess it.

In our resilience assessment we ask the following questions to help you determine where you fall.

1. I often wake up feeling tired.

         __ Never   __ Sometimes   __ Always

2. I have trouble falling asleep at night.

         __ Never   __ Sometimes   __ Always

3. I feel drowsy or even drift off to sleep during the day.

         __ Never   __ Sometimes   __ Always

4. I have low levels of energy and/or significant drops in energy during the day.

         __ Never   __ Sometimes   __ Always

Pretty simple. It turns out the best determinate of how well you are sleeping is how drowsy you are during the day. A real indicator that you need to improve your sleep is if you are drifting off to sleep during movies, in the car (hopefully not while driving), etc. Once you have assessed your sleep, please take a moment to immerse yourself in this content, and more importantly, at the end, choose one small thing you will do to enhance your sleep thereby jump-starting your resilience almost immediately.

Ready?

Why are we starting the Physical Mastery section with sleep? Because **getting adequate sleep makes you more emotionally, physically, mentally, and spiritually resilient.** It impacts directly on just about every aspect of your body and your life. And while the impact of exercise or diet can often take weeks or months to be felt, the impact of changes in sleep are immediate. If you sleep well one night, you'll feel it the next morning.

DANGERS OF SLEEP DEPRIVATION

(Note to those who may have grappled with insomnia, you get to skip ahead to sleep strategy 1 on page 86.)

Not getting enough sleep is linked with many chronic diseases and conditions, such as diabetes, heart disease, obesity and depression.
–Centre for Disease Control and Prevention

For those of you who still need convincing, according to former executive director of the Division of Sleep Medicine at Harvard Medical School, Russel Sanna, sleep deprivation is the new normal in Western society, much like smoking was in the 1950s, and it is a globally recognized health crisis.

Did you know that approximately two-thirds of North Americans undersleep and undervalue sleep? God, I value sleep so much now! But did you know that we sleep about three hours less per day than what was the norm prior to the Industrial Revolution? I find that to be a lot. Hectic lives, caffeine, artificial light, and screen time are all major contributing factors to our limited sleep, which makes sense. The result is that sleep deprivation now rivals obesity and smoking as our greatest public health crisis.

It is an issue that affects the health and productivity of nations, and as such, both governments and corporations are starting to take notice.

SLEEP DEPRIVATION SHOULD NOT BE TAKEN LIGHTLY

This is the section that is not good for me to focus on, but it's a motivation for those of you who can sleep but choose to do other things like work, watch TV, play video games, and just enjoy life, which I totally get. So, here is your motivation to get your butts to bed!

1. Those who are sleep deprived have an increased risk for illness.

When you don't get enough sleep, your immune system does not function optimally and inflammatory proteins and blood sugar levels rise in response to lower levels of insulin being released throughout the night. All of these negative effects on the body contribute to an increased risk of diabetes, heart disease, stroke, and infection.

2. You are more susceptible to stress without a good night's sleep.

You are more likely to struggle with your emotions when sleep deprived. Without sufficient rest, you may have trouble keeping your emotions in check. Increased feelings of irritability, anxiety, sadness, depression, and anger are common. I totally relate to this. I just cannot regulate my emotions as well when I'm exhausted.

3. Another side effect of lack of sleep is weight gain.

Leptin, a hormone that helps regulate energy balances, is impaired when you are sleep deprived. Since leptin plays an important role in appetite control and metabolism, having low levels of this hormone results in hunger not being naturally suppressed. Therefore, your appetite and cravings increase. I cannot tell you how much I crave carbs when I do not sleep well. My sister, a TV broadcaster who often gets up at 3 a.m. for the morning show, says she dreams of bagels and bread and muffins on the days she is up so early. This is a real thing.

4. Your performance declines with lack of sleep.

There are measurable reductions in brain activity that occur after a period of sleep deprivation. When you do not get a sufficient amount of sleep, your mental performance suffers, impairing your ability to process new information and memories impacting your overall mood, focus, and high-level cognitive function. Yup!

5. Finally, when you are exhausted, both physically and mentally, there is an increased risk of injury, errors, and accidents.

This tired state of mind may lead to mishaps like stubbing your toe, cutting yourself in the kitchen, or getting into a car accident.

Sleep deprivation is dangerous. A strange but funny fact is that Guinness World Records no longer tracks the longest period without sleep, as it is considered too dangerous an activity to engage in. Incidentally, sword swallowing and glass eating are okay.

BEWARE OF FALSE SOLUTIONS

When it comes to sleep, we have really lost touch with our bodily senses. We have been taught culturally to push ourselves and drive through. Some also see sleepiness or lack of energy as a weakness and/or as a need for fuel: such as a need for caffeine, sugar, and high-glycemic foods, as opposed to what you really need, which is rest. Strangely, many of us fight rest, perhaps finding being sleepy still triggering. My yoga teachers noted that whenever they assign "rest" as a remedy for an ailment, students fight it.

Avoid caffeine in the afternoon and certainly within at least six hours of sleep to avoid any negative effects from it. I already shared that I had to give up coffee all together. I now drink matcha lattes, which I love. Although matcha has caffeine in it, it also contains high levels of the amino acid L-theanine, which stimulates the production of "calming" neurotransmitters that enhance concentration and mood and actually promote sleep. It's a bonus that matcha doesn't give you the jitters the way that coffee does.

Don't use alcohol as a sleep aid. I tried that and it did not work. I even tried alcohol with CBD oil; that also did not work. It did make me more tired, in some instances I even fell asleep, but then I woke up in an hour or two. Some people are tempted to use alcohol from time to time as a sleep promoter. While it is true that alcohol makes most people sleepy, myself included, and therefore increases the speed of sleep onset, the problem is that alcohol disrupts the foundational structure of sleep, particularly during the second part of the night.

Avoid sleeping pills. I tried all of the over-the-counter sleep aids. I am not alone, though, as sleep aid consumption is on the rise. Just for fun, I did a quick search on Amazon for sleeping pills and 645 different pills came up—wowzers. We, as a society, are clearly struggling with sleep, but I think the thing to remember is that sleep aids are medications, and like most medications, they often have side effects. We can also become addicted, and the more I read about them, the more I learned they did not allow you to enter the deepest state of sleep, so you would still wake up groggy and tired.

Here's the good news—there are ways to improve the quality and quantity of sleep naturally. But before we go there, let's answer the most common sleep question I get when I teach this: How much sleep do we actually need?

This is tricky. The Sleep Institute says that adults need to get seven to nine hours of sleep per night consistently to function well. Any more or less, they say, also increases your risk for serious conditions like diabetes, heart disease, and even death.

Adequate sleep, they share, is also essential to peak performance. And yes, in fact, I have learned that we grow neurons in our brains when we sleep. These neurons connect with other neurons in our body, allowing us to encode new learning, movement patterns, and memories.

When working with my insomnia coach, however, he was very firm in sharing that recent research actually suggests differently and that many adults can maintain their performance and health through getting five and a half hours of good quality or core sleep. He referred to studies of college students who were actually restricted to that amount of sleep for a period of several months and their performance in school did not decline. He also mentioned a similar study with surgeons, which sounds pretty risky for their patients. They were actually going through their residency and performed successfully despite the five and a half hours they slept on average.

I share this because there is no one answer here. As Joshua Rosenthal, the Founder of the Institute for Integrative Nutrition, where I studied health coaching, always repeated, "We are all bio-individual." So you have to go back to those questions I asked you earlier to determine whether you are getting sufficient quantity and quality of sleep for YOU.

The key to keep in mind is that NOT all sleep is created equally. Meaning that many of us end up getting far too little of the deep restorative rest that *really* boosts our performance, even if we're "technically" sleeping seven or eight hours a night.

THERE ARE FIVE STAGES OF SLEEP

Scientists categorized the stages of sleep based on the characteristics of the brain and body during sleep.

Each sleep stage serves a unique role in brain and body restoration.

There are many sleep studies that have demonstrated that depriving subjects of specific sleep stages of the sleep cycle has an adverse effect

THE 5 STAGES OF SLEEP

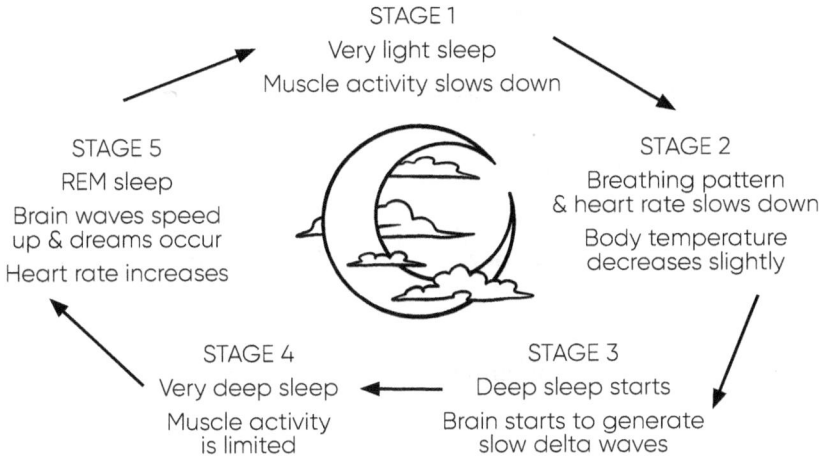

STAGE 1
Very light sleep
Muscle activity slows down

STAGE 5
REM sleep
Brain waves speed
up & dreams occur
Heart rate increases

STAGE 2
Breathing pattern
& heart rate slows down
Body temperature
decreases slightly

STAGE 4
Very deep sleep
Muscle activity
is limited

STAGE 3
Deep sleep starts
Brain starts to generate
slow delta waves

on body and brain functions. Deep sleep and very deep sleep are particularly important. During deep sleep your body releases growth hormones and repairs muscles, tissues, and bones. This stage of sleep also enhances the immune system and regulates glucose metabolism. Additionally, it is critical for brain function and memory formation.

So now we know that we need quality and a consistent quantity of sleep that is right for us, but how do we actually do this?

Although we can't control sleep as I brutally experienced, we can control perpetuating factors leading to poor sleep. My research has revealed ten strategies for dealing with these perpetuating factors and ultimately optimizing our sleep. No one is expecting you to implement all ten. These are sleep-enhancing best practices. I share them so that you may experiment and find strategies that are most effective for you. In fact, I will ask you to only choose one to start. Remember our discussion on the ONE thing? Recall also that the need for quality deep sleep is common sense. But is it common practice?

SLEEP STRATEGY 1: Design a relaxing bedtime routine

Engaging in a pre-bedtime routine is beneficial for several reasons. Humans are creatures of habit, and once well-learned sequences of behaviors are established, one action usually automatically stimulates the next.

Anyone know (or remember) how to get a baby to sleep?

You don't have to be a parent to understand. How do you get a baby to sleep? You bathe them, moisturize them, massage them, read them a book (even though they don't understand), nurse them or give them a bottle with lights down low, sing a song. There's a specific routine—and that routine is key. If you don't follow it, what happens? First, your baby likely won't fall asleep. And second, if they do, you may be woken up by a crying baby at 3 a.m. Well, we are big babies! The same things happen to us when we do not follow a nice, soothing, predictable bedtime routine. When instead you watch Netflix, answer emails at 11 p.m. in bed, or scroll Instagram, your mind races. When you then shut off the lights and expect to fall asleep, your mind and body are disconnected. Your body may be tired, but your mind is wired and you cannot sleep. I must acknowledge again that there are lucky people like my husband who is built from a different cloth and can watch horror movies in bed and then fall soundly asleep while I watch him with amazement and envy. Remember, we are all bioindividual.

In general, your bedtime routine should serve to ease the transition from waking state to sleep state with a period of relaxing activities an hour or so before bed. Just like a baby. Consider taking a bath (the rise, then fall in body temperature promotes drowsiness), read a book, drink some calming "sleepy time" tea or warm almond milk and cinnamon, which is also good and highly recommended by my yoga teachers. Basically, you are trying to send a signal to your central nervous system that all is well, you are safe, that it is time to relax. Gentle, restorative yoga, with a focus on long exhales, is so helpful.

The key is that through a calm, peaceful, consistent sleep routine we are ensuring that we tap into that parasympathetic nervous system. Remember in the neuroscience section we spoke about it? The parasympathetic nervous system is the rest, digest, and detoxify branch. We cannot sleep when we are in the sympathetic nervous system, which is our arousal system designed to keep us awake so we don't get eaten by a bear. This is also where I was making a mistake; in trying to sleep and thinking about all the dangers of sleep deprivation, I was actually putting myself in this sympathetic state, which by no coincidence is also called the arousal system. Letting go of the effort to sleep and having a solid sleep routine was and continues to be key, for me anyway.

SLEEP STRATEGY 2: Don't nap during the day

Sorry, this is a tough one I learned from my insomnia CBT therapist. He taught me the principle of sleep pressure or sleep drive. Essentially, the principle is that the longer you are awake and the more active you are, the greater the natural pressure to sleep will be.

He explained to me that a more intense pressure to sleep leads to more intense sleep. By definition then, if you nap, you decrease your pressure to sleep. Interestingly, he also warned about going to bed too early and sleeping in too late because it disrupts our circadian rhythm, also known as the sleep–wake cycle. So, you can imagine, this really sucked for me. I got used to having a midday meditation, which often turned into a nap. It would reset me for the late afternoon and evening, but then I could not sleep at night. Ugh. I even started doing meditations sitting up to get the restoration without impacting the sleep pressure. But seriously, if you are having trouble sleeping, it seems counterintuitive, but no naps!

SLEEP STRATEGY 3: Create a quiet, dark, and comfortable sleep environment

The right sleep environment is crucial for the best possible sleep. Although complete environmental control may be difficult to achieve, especially when traveling or with a snoring mate like my hubby, everything that can be controlled should be controlled. Make sure the room is dark with a comfortable temperature (around 19 degrees Celsius / 66 degrees Fahrenheit is best). It's better to have the room slightly cooler than normal with enough bed covers to stay warm. If you are really hot at night or perimenopausal with a tendency toward night sweats, you can consider purchasing a cooling mattress pad that regulates temperature and prevents you from sleeping hot.

Another issue is light. We have a streetlamp in front of our bedroom window, so I wear an eye mask. I tried so many and finally discovered that the soft silk ones worked best for me. Our street can be loud at times, as can the sounds of snoring or my dog scratching himself. So we moved the dog out of the room, and aside from one night where he left evidence of rebellion in the living room, it has been fine. I did not move my husband to the living room, though. I began wearing earplugs. A friend told me you can have custom ones created, but I just bought mine at a drugstore. It takes a while to get used to them, but they work. You can also use a fan or noise-canceling machine. We have an air filter that does the job. Essentially, you want to keep surrounding sound levels steady, low, and consistent.

SLEEP STRATEGY 4: Stick to a consistent wake-up time and bedtime every day of the week

While many believe sleeping in on the weekends is a luxury that should not be missed, this habit creates body clock disruptions that can turn into chronic sleep problems. I know this one is hard to follow. There is nothing better than waking up and realizing you don't have to get out of bed and then dozing off again. It feels so good, but someone who regularly wakes up at 6 a.m. on most days, then sleeps until 9 a.m. on weekends, is readjusting their body's internal clock for two days every week. Basically, if you live in Toronto, it's like flying to Vancouver each weekend. You'll get jetlagged.

The delayed wake-up time leads to later daylight exposure and an alteration in your sleep pressure. This ultimately pushes back the next sleep period. Come Sunday night you may feel inclined to stay up later or have a hard time falling asleep early—and when the alarm clock sounds early Monday morning, you feel like you're still on West Coast time and your body is determined to sleep another few hours. As a result, you fall out of sync and may feel fatigued, moody, less alert, and find it hard to concentrate and show up as your best.

CIRCADIAN RHYTHM/SLEEP CYCLE

It is part of your body's clock, informing you when the best time to sleep and wake is. However, like any other system in the body, it can get out of balance.

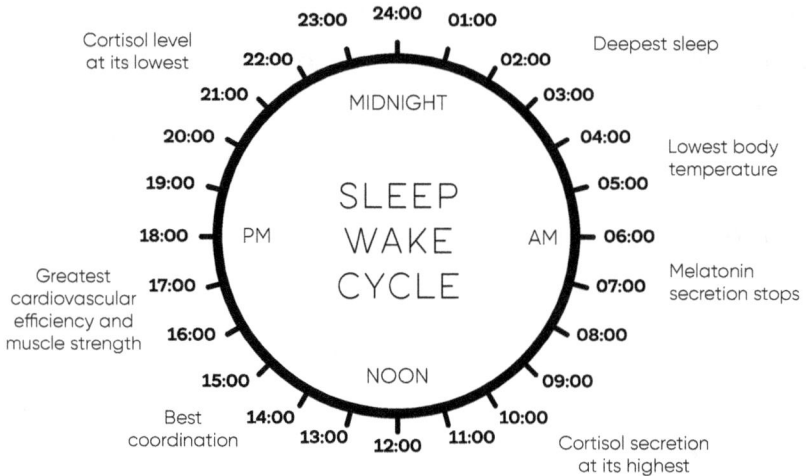

So try to stick to a regular sleeping schedule throughout the week and see what happens. It's not fun or indulgent, but it may make a huge difference.

SLEEP STRATEGY 5: Limit your use of screens and artificial light at night

This is a big one, and one that will get a lot of resistance—turn off electronics, such as computers, phones, and tablets at least one hour before bedtime and keep them out of the bedroom. Yup, I'm really not going to win a popularity contest here. And if you are not feeling the pain of non-sleep, you may not feel like implementing this. These devices suppress the production of the sleep-inducing hormone melatonin.

This sleep strategy is a difficult one because so many of us have a habit of reading or watching shows on a device in bed. To get around this, I initially used a screen-darkening application that can be downloaded onto a computer or tablet. I also use blue-light–blocking glasses that eliminate the negative impact of screen light on our sleep. They look pretty funny, but fortunately nobody but my family sees them.

The additional (online) resources have links to both the free app called F.lux, which adapts the color of your computer's display to the time of day, and to the blue-light–blocking glasses I find work best.

I use them when there is an emergency and I absolutely have to look at a screen. I think shutting everything down is so important symbolically, too, and disconnects us from the external world. It also ensures we do not stimulate our nervous system whether that be through a show, the news, or just daily life.

SLEEP STRATEGY 6: Don't go to bed on a full stomach

We know a family, I am not even joking, who makes sandwiches before bed to eat if they wake up at night. It is no surprise they are overweight and sluggish all the time. Eating too close to bedtime can raise your core body temperature and metabolic rate, making it difficult to fall asleep and stay asleep.

Eating a pizza at 10 p.m. may be a literal recipe for insomnia. Ideally, finish dinner several hours before bedtime. I close the kitchen, meaning I don't eat after 7 p.m. most days, and avoid foods that cause indigestion. If you get hungry at night, snack on foods that (in your experience) won't disturb your sleep, perhaps a piece of fruit or some nuts.

When Aubrey and I started eating our dinner with the kids, we moved dinnertime ahead by about ninety minutes. Not only did we feel better not going to bed on a full stomach, I also noticed that I lost five pounds just through this one act. There's plenty of data, while not appearing conclusive, that does suggest that weight loss and enhanced sleep are benefits of eating earlier in the evening.

SLEEP STRATEGY 7: Expose yourself to lots of bright natural light during the day

Exposure to natural light during the day, particularly in the morning hours, will reinforce the body's natural circadian sleep–wake cycle. Light is important because it serves as the major synchronizer of something called your master clock. Other biological clocks throughout your body in turn synchronize to your master clock.

To maintain and anchor your master clock, you want to get bright outdoor light exposure for 30–60 minutes a day, ideally at noon or before (and ideally without sunglasses). I remember early in my career working for the federal government sitting in a cubicle away from the window. It could have been the nature of the work, which I found excruciatingly dull, or it could have been the lack of air circulation, but I blamed the lack of natural light. Without it, my plant was dying and so was I. We both did better after I left that job. The point is we are like plants and need light. I know this is not always possible when we are at work during the day, especially for those of us living in a cold northern climate where the days are very short and nights long. But try to get outside at lunch.

I also rented a very cool red-light lamp for a while. Red-light therapy is a simple way to expose your body to more natural light and help reset your circadian clock.

SLEEP STRATEGY 8: Exercise regularly and ideally early in the day

Exercise can help you fall asleep faster and sleep more soundly when done early in the day. I used to exercise in the evening after dinner and was way too pumped up. Exercise stimulates the body to secrete the stress hormone cortisol. Cortisol activates the alerting mechanism in the brain. That is actually great in the morning or midday but sucks when you're trying to fall asleep. A good guide to follow is to work out earlier in the day, or to finish exercising at least three hours before bed. When I speak of exercising, I mean more vigorous workouts. I walk each evening with the dog, which is great, and restorative yoga, as I mentioned earlier, is wonderful for sleep. Save the high-intensity heart-pumping workout for the morning.

SLEEP STRATEGY 9: Resolve dilemmas outside of the bedroom

Not surprisingly, worrying can make it hard to fall asleep. Although I do not like to admit to it, I am a worrywart (I just noticed how odd that expression is). I have a tendency to worry and just like worrying about not sleeping can lead to more non-sleep, worrying in general causes stress and anxiety and can activate that arousal system we spoke of earlier, which disrupts our sleep.

So to sleep faster, better, deeper, we need to learn how to let go of our worries and not bring them into the bedroom. For the record, I am not encouraging suppressing worrying thoughts, as that can be equally stressful. When I "try" to not think about something, inevitably I think more about it. Like in mindfulness training, it is easier to notice the thought, acknowledge it, then gently ask it to leave or try to plan for this. I know that sounds funny.

This is an exercise/tool I received from my CBT therapist. It is called Constructive Thinking. He suggested doing this in early evening or during the day, but not before bed. The idea is that you actually think of and write down the three or more worries you have that are most likely to keep you up at night. You then brainstorm solutions or things that you may do to help you resolve the worries tomorrow or at a set date. Finally, write your to-do list for the next day. The to-dos may be entirely separate from the worries you listed, you just want to note them for yourself.

Now, if you get into bed and find yourself thinking about one of your worries or what you have to do the next day, you can tell yourself you already dealt with it. What helps me as well is to then Ishvara Pranidhana it. Remember that one? It means to surrender the worry to the Highest Source.

Resolving your daily dilemmas outside of the bedroom also means avoiding stressful or stimulating activities like doing work or discussing emotional issues with your partner in bed. Instead, write down things you are grateful for, listen to or think of something funny, or meditate.

SLEEP STRATEGY 10: Meditate

Other than hibernating bears, meditators are apparently the world's best sleepers.

We will explore mindfulness and meditation further in the self-awareness section, but for now know the research shows that mediation is great for sleep. A recent study published in the Harvard Health Blog demonstrated that mindfulness meditation helps fight insomnia and improves sleep.

There are several reasons for why meditation has such a positive impact upon our sleep:

1. Meditation helps to shift our body from the sympathetic (stress response) to the parasympathetic relaxation response we spoke of earlier. Often insomnia arises as a result of stress, anxiety, and worry. Meditation helps focus and calm the hyperactive mind. It also lowers cortisol, the stress hormone.

2. Meditation before bed boosts melatonin levels. Melatonin is a powerful neurochemical critical to the falling asleep process. It also increases serotonin, which is a precursor to melatonin.

3. Finally, meditation has been shown to reduce the heart rate and trigger the parts of the brain responsible for sleep.

You can use a guided sleep meditation. There are many available on YouTube or the Insight Timer app. You can also try to use your own breath to meditate. I like this, as it does not require me to rely on my phone, and if I wake up at night, I always have my breath to turn to. My yoga teachers often say, **"If the breath is calm, so goes the mind."**

Try this tonight: When you get into bed, lie on your back and get really comfy. Then bring your attention to your breath. Notice the cool air coming in and the warm air leaving. When your mind wanders away from your breath, bring it back. Once you do this a few times, start to double your exhale by holding after the exhale. This is known as a relaxing breath ratio, and it triggers your para-sympathetic nervous system.

Try this now so you will know what to do tonight:

Inhale to the count of four, exhale for four, and pause for four. Repeat this at least twelve times. If four feels too short you can try it with a 5–5–5 ratio or whatever ratio feels comfortable.

As I come to a conclusion here, it is also important to note that notwithstanding all these strategies, going to bed early is a great starting point to a better night's sleep. I remember being told as a child that one hour before midnight is like two after midnight.

Benjamin Franklin's famous quote nicely motivates us as well: "Early to bed, early to rise, makes a man healthy, wealthy, and wise."

Now it's time to Do the Work and BE Resilient

Review the challenge exercise following this lesson and take some time to design your sleep. Make a decision about how much sleep you would like to get and then identify ONE thing you will incorporate in your sleep routine for the next two weeks or hopefully beyond. Often the smaller change is better, so your habit-change alarms don't go off.

In case you are curious, I created the dark, comfortable sleeping environment (including kicking out the dog) and got all the props. I did that one as it did not require habit change. Then I started with eliminating the blue light. I also bought blue-light–blocking glasses to help me when I just could not avoid it. It made a huge difference—I started getting really sleepy wearing them.

Remember, no one is going to do this for you. Identify your barriers to sleeping better, commit to yourself, and as my yoga teachers say, "See what happens."

THE SLEEP DEEP CHALLENGE

Review the ten strategies to enhance sleep and identify at least ONE that you will incorporate into your routine for the duration of the program. If you are not feeling some benefit after two weeks, feel free to modify the practice.

1. Design a relaxing bedtime routine.
2. Don't nap during the day.
3. Create a quiet, dark environment.
4. Stick to a consistent bedtime and wake-up time.

5. Limit use of screens within one hour of bedtime.
6. Avoid eating within three hours of bedtime.
7. Get lots of natural light during the day.
8. Exercise early and regularly.
9. Resolve daily dilemmas outside of the bedroom.
10. Meditate.

Finally, I have some additional learning material on our website. It has some great articles and videos in support of the information provided in this lesson. The links to the free apps I referred to are also included there. Use the QR code at the back of the book to access the site.

The last word on sleeping deep:
Make sleep a priority.

Chapter 6

EAT CONSCIOUSLY

Food is not just calories, it is information. It talks to your DNA and tells it what to do. The most powerful tool to change your health, environment, and entire world is your fork.

–Dr. Mark Hyman

In this chapter, we are exploring one of my favorite topics and a key component of Physical Mastery: healthy eating. Who knew that good old-fashioned healthy eating could make us resilient to the ups and downs of life? Well, it can, and quite significantly so.

When my girls were little, they could not understand why I would not buy them ice cream bars and chips or even fruit roll-ups. (By the way, check out the ingredients in fruit roll-ups and you'll note that fruit is not a major ingredient, but corn syrup, dried corn syrup, sugar, and partially hydrogenated cottonseed oil are.) They would constantly beg me to buy them junk food, so I used the analogy of the houses in the *Three Little Pigs* fable.

The story, if you recall, begins with the pigs' mother sending her three little ones out to the world to build houses for themselves. The first little pig, who according to the story was "lazy," built his house quickly and easily out of straw. Much to his dismay, a wolf showed up and blew it down. The second little pig put in slightly more time and effort and built a house out of sticks. This house, while sturdier, was also blown down by the wolf; though, it took more huffing and puffing. The third little pig, on the other hand, worked hard all day and built his house out of bricks, which the wolf could not blow down, as hard as he tried.

I then said to the girls, "Your body is your house. What do you want to build it out of?"

They totally got it. They didn't like it, but they understood that we are made out of the "materials" we choose to put in, and it takes more effort to build a strong house. While this sounds simplistic, I think we can all agree that the better we eat, the better we feel and the more energy and stamina we have to perform at our highest level. Plus, research suggests that a healthier body means a healthier brain and a longer life. And we could all use that.

WHAT YOU WILL DISCOVER

The goal of this chapter is to discover why eating consciously is critical, not only for your resilience, but for your overall health. It is also to empower you to make positive dietary changes, new habits that will actually stick. Specifically, in this section:

- We will look at the impact of our modern diet on energy, productivity, and disease.

- I will share five keys to eating consciously, including the basics of clean eating.

- We will finish by exploring the benefits of mindful eating.

Before I get into the "meat and potatoes" of eating, first a bit to provide extra motivation. Let's look at where we are at as a society. We are in the midst of a health crisis, and I am not referring to any viral pandemic. Rates of obesity, diabetes, and chronic disease are at an all-time high in North America, according to the Center for Disease Control (CDC) and Lancet Study, as well as Statistics Canada.

If we care to acknowledge it or not, there is a health epidemic in Canada. According to Stats Can:

- 61.8 percent of all adult males are currently overweight.
- 46.2 percent of adult females are currently overweight.
- 70 percent of males between the ages of 45 and 64 are overweight.
- 54 percent of women between the ages of 45 and 64 are overweight.

Given these statistics, it's not surprising that Diabetes Canada predicts that the number of people with diabetes in Canada will rise from 3.4 million in 2015 to 5 million in 2025. This is a 44 percent increase.

If that isn't scary enough, according to the 2015 Canadian Cancer Statistics, over the course of the last twenty years, the number of new cases of cancer has increased by 65 percent on a per capita basis. The number of new cancer cases in Canada is expected to rise about 40 percent in the next fifteen years.

I share all these alarming stats with you because when you are sick, you lack energy, can't perform at your peak, and don't feel very resilient at all. Also, I share them because there is a way to reverse this trend and take hold of your well-being. I have learned this both in theory and practice and want to empower you to do the same.

Dr. David Katz, one of the instructors in the health coaching and nutrition school I studied at, said repeatedly, "Most diseases are not random occurrences but the consequences of the things people do every day." Diseases are not causes; diseases are the effects.

I really love that! It puts more power back into our hands.

Longitudinal research has now proven that the way you take care of yourself, namely how well you eat, sleep, and move, will determine your health and well-being and life expectancy.

So there is a direct correlation between the modern diet and health. And yet most of us do not live like we are accountable for our health and well-being at all. The modern Standard American Diet causes nutrition deficiency and leads to obesity, hypertension, hyperlipidemia, diabetes, and cancer. Conversely, an increasing number of studies have shown the contribution of nourishing foods to a healthy body and immune system.

Let's clarify what we mean by the Standard American Diet.

Standard American Diet (SAD) is a modern dietary pattern that is generally characterized as being:

- High in fried food and unhealthy processed fats
- High in processed meat such as bacon and deli meats
- High in processed sugar and sugar-laden drinks
- High in refined grains such as white flour

- High in chemicals and pesticides
- Low in fiber
- Low in complex carbohydrates
- Low in plant-based foods
- Extremely high in processed or industrialized foods

A study published in *The American Journal of Clinical Nutrition* found that the average American gets 61 percent of their calories from highly processed foods. In other words, the typical American diet is dominated by processed, factory-made food-like products that didn't even exist a hundred years ago.

I actually think that 61 percent is a very conservative number. Other sources, including Melanie Warner, a former food industry reporter and author of the book *Pandora's Lunchbox: How Processed Food Took Over the American Meal,* say 70 percent of our calories now come from processed food. She beautifully illustrates that we value convenience over health when it comes to food.

What I find interesting is that everywhere modern processed foods go, chronic diseases like obesity, type 2 diabetes, and heart disease follow.

The research demonstrates that when people abandon their traditional foods in favor of the SAD diet, they get sick. So it is clearly not genetics but food. For example, Indigenous people have patterns of illness very different from Western civilization, yet they rapidly developed Western disease patterns once exposed to Western foods and lifestyles.

WHAT IS A HEALTHY DIET?

One of the challenges even the best-intentioned healthy eater has is trying to determine what a healthy diet actually is. We are bombarded with confusing and often conflicting recommendations, which often overlap with diet trends. I have heard (and at times, followed) all the following advice on each of these food groups:

- FAT: low fat, high fat, no saturated fat, no fat at all, only "good fat" such as olive oil
- CARBS: more whole grains and complex carbs, no grains, zero carbs
- MEAT: "where's the beef," no meat, less-fatty meat, no red meat, only grass-fed beef, "beyond meat"
- DAIRY: "milk does your body good," dairy is hazardous to your health, organic, hormone-free milk, milk replacements such as almond and oat milk
- EGGS: "get crackin'," no eggs, one egg a day, egg whites only, unlimited pasture-raised organic eggs
- FRUIT: more fruit, less fruit, no fruit at all, only organic fruit on an empty stomach
- SUGAR: sugar is fine, sugar will kill you, sugar is a drug and additive, use artificial sweeteners, avoid all artificial sweeteners, use natural sugars like honey and maple syrup, use stevia, munk fruit, and sugar alcohols such as xylitol instead

Whoa! I need to do the overwhelm audit after this. There is so much confusing information, and the cynic in me points to the fact that a lot of it comes from the various food associations paying for marketing and funding media.

This makes knowing what to eat (for ourselves and our kids) difficult and navigating a supermarket stressful. Where do you start?

KEYS TO EATING CONSCIOUSLY

I would like to simplify what to eat and not eat for you by sharing with you my five keys to eating consciously. As I shared earlier, I studied at the world's largest nutrition school in New York called the Institute for Integrative Nutrition (IIN), and it was there that my eyes were opened to many of these ideas. My mom also always cooked everything from scratch, and to this day, much of the food we consume with my parents is from their huge, robust garden. Thank you, Mama!

KEY 1: You are what you eat, so don't be fast, cheap, easy, or fake

We are quite literally what we eat. This is one of those things that is common knowledge but not common practice. Next to breathing, eating is likely our most vital bodily function. To create a healthy body and mind, our food must be nourishing. Remember, we are building our house here!

There are thousands of peer-reviewed studies that prove there is a direct link between what you put in your mouth and your energy levels, mental wellness and agility, immune system performance, and overall health. How you eat will ultimately play into how resilient you are.

Peak performers, like Olympians, follow a strict diet because food gives them strength, energy, and stamina. It gives them good health and makes them strong.

Dr. Mark Hyman says that food is information. "Real, whole foods contain information in the form of vitamins, minerals, carbohydrates, fats, protein, phytonutrients, and fiber. These compounds impact every node of the Functional Medicine matrix, like our vascular and immune systems, detox and energy pathways, microbiome, and everything in between."

Joshua Rosenthal, the founder of IIN, said that when you eat junky and processed food, your organs, muscles, body, and even your thoughts ultimately become junky and processed.

If that isn't motivation enough, my yoga teachers often say, "Nothing tastes as good as health."

KEY 2: Eat like your great-great-grandmother

One hundred years ago, all we ate was local, organic food, grass-fed meat, if any, and real, whole plant foods. There were no fast-food restaurants, there was no junk food, there was no frozen food—there was just what you made.

And most meals were eaten at home. In the modern age, that tradition and that knowledge is being lost.

While at the IIN, we looked at over 100 diets, and many of them seemed contradictory. Vegan vs. paleo is a great example of that. Vegans believe animal products cause chronic disease and that a diet high in veggies, fruits, and grains is best. Paleos like veggies too, but think that grass-fed and wild meats are important for health, and they believe that grains, starches, and sugars are the real health-killers.

Yet the advocates of both diets swear improved health on them. So how is this possible?

What I began to see is that the diets that have positive impact, such as the vegan and paleo diets, have one thing in common and that is that they consist largely of REAL, non-industrialized food.

So when I say eat like your great-great-grandmother, what I mean is **eat single-ingredient items, real foods, cooked at home, as often as possible, just like your great-great-grandmother would have.** This entails embracing whole foods and shopping like a detective. Grocery stores have become labyrinths of temptation.

Embrace real, fresh, whole food.

What does that mean in practice? We are speaking about enjoying real, fresh foods that come directly from nature with minimal processing:

- Leafy greens
- Veggies
- Fruit
- Raw nuts and seeds
- Healthy fats
- Gluten-free grains (if tolerated)
- Limited organic dairy (if tolerated)

In other words, we're talking about a mostly plant-based diet with limited meat, dairy, and highly processed grains. In terms of the meat we eat, it should be sustainably farmed, ideally organic, and the fish should be wild caught.

But don't we need more protein? I can hear some of you protesting already. A good friend of mine is vegetarian and has explained this to me very well. While we do need some protein, perhaps we don't need as much as we might think. The CDC and Physician's Committee for Responsible Medicine (PCRM) both agree that protein deficiency is not a problem in our society. In fact, the PCRM even says that we actually get too much protein, around double of what we really need.

I have created a Conscious Eating Guide for you. It includes sources and links to further information. It takes a lot of time to do your research, so I have done it for you and the links are there for you to explore further if you like.

Shop like a detective.

Eating like our great-great-grandmothers in the twenty-first century requires us to shop intelligently and strategically.

1. **Plan ahead.** Grocery stores are filled with items packaged and advertised to make you want them, and if you show up without a plan, there is a good chance you will leave with some of these products. To avoid overstocking your cart and choosing unhealthy food options, first create a detailed shopping list based on what you want to eat throughout the week. Making a weekly menu can be really helpful. And don't shop when you're hungry.

2. **Read the ingredients list.** Forget the white box of "nutrition facts" on the back of packaged products and look straight to the ingredient list. This is where you can learn if a food product is healthy or harmful. Notice a long list of ingredients with words that you cannot pronounce? Put it back. If your grandma wouldn't recognize the ingredients, then you shouldn't be eating

it. Instead, choose one-item foods (i.e., an apple) or products with short ingredient lists that contain all recognizable food ingredients.

3. **Shop the perimeter.** I think we've all heard this: the freshest foods (like produce and meats) are kept on the perimeter of the store, leaving all the processed junk in the middle aisles. Avoid temptation all together and stick to the perimeter, only traveling to the inner aisles for specific items.

Also, consider farmers' markets, fruit stands, and organic delivery boxes.

KEY 3: Crowd out "food-like products," a.k.a. processed food

The idea of giving up foods that you're used to eating or love eating turns many people off from making positive dietary changes. We don't like change, and those habits are instilled deeply in our limbic brain.

Even with following your great-great-grandmother's diet, it can be hard for people to adjust to cutting out all those convenient, processed foods. So I am not saying never ever eat the following foods. The most important thing to do, in my opinion, is just to start learning how to replace fake foods (listed below) with real foods. In other words, I am suggesting you fill yourself with the real healthy foods and thereby leave little space for—or crowd out—the following:

All processed/industrialized food

- Refined sugars
- Trans fats
- Food products that come in boxes, cans, and wrappers

The healthiest diets, as I mentioned earlier, all have one thing in common—the foods they recommend avoiding. Staying away from all processed/industrialized food will positively help your health the most.

Sugar Blues

Now here is a big one. We all know sugar is bad, and I often hear a little bit is okay. But what is a little bit?

The body can handle, as in metabolize, up to a very maximum of six teaspoons of added sugar per day. The problem is that most people consume a lot more than that. Sugar is not only present in foods that taste very sweet, it is in everything it seems. Most Americans consume well over three times that amount, with teens and men munching on the largest amounts. The result is chaos, stress, and overload for the body.

Researchers have found that sugar inhibits our immune system; disturbs the mineral balance in our bodies; can cause fertility issues; accelerates aging; is a major contributor to diabetes; is connected with the development of various forms of cancer including but not limited to breast, ovarian, prostate, lung, and stomach cancer; and it causes a rapid rise in adrenaline, as well as hyperactivity, anxiety, and loss of concentration in kids and adults alike. Finally, consuming sugar has the effect of causing spikes in blood sugar levels, which cause the body to generate more cortisol. Cortisol is the stress hormone we covered earlier and is best known for its involvement in the fight or flight response, causing a temporary increase in energy production while limiting normal organ function and higher brain function.

If that isn't enough, refined sugar is a highly addictive drug. In fact, laboratory studies on rats suggest sugar is more addictive than cocaine.

Check out *146 Reasons to Avoid Sugar* for a comprehensive list. If you have a sweet tooth, like me, print it out and tape it to your pantry cupboard.

KEY 4: Cook more often

I can hear you groaning already. Who has time to cook—especially after a long day at work?

We complain about not having enough time to cook, but according to Dr. Hyman, North Americans spend more time watching cooking on the Food Network than actually preparing their own meals. I believe him. I had a client who had many beautiful cookbooks but never cooked. She just read them.

Overly scheduled, hectic lives and single-parent homes coupled with the ease, availability, and affordability of fast food have hijacked our dinner table. According to stats from Dr. Hyman again:

- In 1900, 2 percent of meals were eaten outside the home in the US.
- In 2010, 50 percent were eaten away from home in the US, and one in five breakfasts was from McDonald's.
- In 2019, according to Stats Canada, more than half of Canadians ate out or bought takeout food at least once a week. Only 8 percent reported not eating out at all for the past month.

Most family meals happen about three times a week, last less than twenty minutes, and are spent watching television or texting while each family member eats a different microwaved "food."

Eating at home = health and happiness.

Here is why you should really care about home cooking and the family table: EVERYTHING good you want for yourself and your family is correlated with eating together around the family dinner table. Research demonstrates that home cooking has many benefits.

Home cooking makes you happier. Not only cooking, but sharing meals with others is associated with greater feelings of happiness as found in an eight-year follow-up of 39,000 people in a cohort from Thailand.

Cooking at home makes you healthier. When you cook, you have more control over what goes into your body. By buying organic, sustainably raised meat, dairy, and produce, you reduce your consumption of highly processed food contaminated by chemical fertilizers, pesticides, hormones, and antibiotics. When you are cooking, chances are you won't add preservatives, artificial flavors and taste enhancers, texturizers, colors, rancid fats, or use toxic packaging. Your portion sizes will likely be smaller as well.

According to research conducted at Harvard University, families who ate together every day or most days had a higher intake of nutrients and vitamins such as calcium, fiber, iron, vitamin B-6, vitamin B-12, vitamin C, and vitamin E; they also had less overall saturated fat intake.

Cooking at home saves money. Eating out or ordering in is expensive, even more than ever before with food prices on the rise. By cutting that costly habit out, your wallet will thank you. According to an article in *Forbes*, it costs almost **five times** as much to order delivery from a restaurant than to cook from scratch. My immigrant father has been saying this my whole life. But it turns out, it's true. Many people opt for the convenience of home-delivered meal kits. Although more affordable and seemingly healthier, they are still almost three times as expensive as when cooking for yourself at home. The *Forbes* researchers found that you will save the most on protein-rich foods, especially high-quality ones, if you buy and prepare them yourself. Expensive entrées with meat are the most expensive to order, but it is the pasta dishes that are most marked up. It is fun to go out, and we all need a break sometimes. Consider starting a dinner club. We did that for many years and found the meals we all served were just as fancy and higher quality than those in the nicest restaurants.

Eating at home makes you thinner. Studies shared by *Medical Daily* have found that eating out led to at least a 50 percent increase in calories, sodium, and total fat consumed.

Eating at home brings you closer with your family and helps kids perform better at school. If you want to do everything you can to ensure your children's well-being, having family home-cooked meals together is a key. According to WebMD, children who eat home-cooked meals more frequently are less likely to be overweight and more likely to have improved health. Fascinatingly, research also shows that children who have regular meals with their parents not only do better in school, but they also have healthier relationships, and they tend to stay out of trouble. Dr. Hyman states they are 42 percent less likely to drink, 50 percent less likely to smoke, and 66 percent less likely to smoke marijuana. Regular family dinners protect girls from bulimia, anorexia, and diet pills. Our dinners are a time to bond. It is the only time in the day where we talk about our day, really connect as a family, and model healthy eating.

Preparing to home cook:

- Free up some time and prepare your pantry for cooking.
- Recognize how much time you spend on social media or watching TV and choose to re-allocate some of that time to preparing meals.
- Readily have the basics on hand so that you can make something without having to go shopping.

Plan ahead:

- My advice is to spend fifteen minutes for meal planning and one hour for shopping on the weekend for success all week long. When I do this I also save money, as I buy the things I need for specific dishes.

- Batch cooking is critical too. I always make more than we need. Leftovers are great for lunches or good to freeze. For example, I triple the recipe for a vegan mac and cheese sauce and freeze it in jars. I can then pull out a jar in the morning and toss with lentil pasta and broccoli. This meal is lovingly known in my house as "Mac and Trees."

KEY 5: Eat mindfully

I couldn't finish a chapter on eating consciously without touching upon the importance of a mindfulness practice called mindful eating.

Have you ever been eating something and suddenly you look down and all the food is gone? The empty plate is there, so you must have gobbled it up without really noticing . . . or smelling, tasting, or enjoying it. That is mindless eating. We often inhale food without even chewing it, and that not only takes the pleasure away from eating, but we also then tend to eat too much and not digest it properly.

Mindfulness, as we will learn later in the book, is about paying attention in the present moment. By extension, mindful eating involves paying full attention to the present experience of eating and drinking. In a way, your object of meditation is your food. You pay full attention to the colors, smells, textures, flavors, temperatures, and even the sounds of eating your food.

It is also about paying attention to how full or hungry you are, which enables us to notice how emotions influence our eating. I used to have a tendency to self-soothe through food (specifically sweets) or emotionally eat. I also had a tendency to overeat and eat when not hungry simply because it was "time to eat" and "dinner was ready." Thanks to mindful eating, I now can notice quickly when something does not sit with me. Lately, my body is not wanting meat, even the highest-quality organic meat. I can now close my eyes and ask myself whether I want to eat something, then get a response. I know that sounds woo-woo, but there is an entire Intuitive Eating movement that basically teaches you to listen to your body, reject fad diets (and diets in general), honor your hunger or lack of it, and take pleasure in your food.

Mindful eating steps and activities

Here is a process and a couple things you can do to become more intentionally present with your eating:

- Take five slow breaths before you eat. Breathe in for the count of four—pause—breathe out for four—pause. Repeat this breathing pattern five times. Recall that through this breathing practice you are tapping into your parasympathetic nervous system or your rest and digest response. If you struggle with digestive issues of any kind, consider doing this before every meal and observe the impact.

- Next, bring attention to your meal, notice how the food looks on your plate, what you will be eating, the colors, textures, arrangement.

- Offer up gratitude for the food and all those involved with getting it on our plate. This is a beautiful, cross-cultural practice that floods you with feel-good emotions.

- Pick up your fork, scoop up some food, and bring it to your nose. Smell it slowly, and notice the saliva created in your mouth as you do so.

- Now, bring the fork to your lips and place the food in your mouth. Resist the urge to bite and swallow just yet. Let the food rest on your tongue for a moment. Once you do so, take a breath and commence to chew. Chew slowly and really taste the flavors. Thích Nhat Hanh used to say, "Drink your food." He advised his students to chew each bite thirty times. It feels a bit excessive for me, but consider seven to ten bites. When

I started doing this I realized I often swallowed my food in big chunks, and now I'm more aware of chewing. Try it and see what happens.

- Put your fork down between each bite of food and focus on chewing. Notice how you feel.

- If you have kids, at dinnertime you may ask everyone to eat in silence for the first few minutes. This was bliss for my husband and me but stressful for my chatty girls, so it might not always work.

- Another good mindful eating activity is to take the first sip of any beverage with full attention. Always remembering to first smell it. Take your first sip of coffee or tea with full attention.

I encourage you to slow down and become more aware of how you eat, when you eat, how much you eat, and how what you eat makes you feel. You may find that this practice alone may change your unconscious eating habits.

Now it's time to Do the Work and BE Resilient

Please visit our website (available via the QR code at the back of the book) to download the Conscious Eating Guide I mentioned earlier. This is a great resource that summarizes what I shared here and provides links to further research.

Next, take on this week's challenge exercise.

THE EAT CONSCIOUSLY CHALLENGE

In the lesson you were introduced to five keys to eating consciously. They are as follows:

1. You are what you eat, so don't be fast, cheap, easy, or fake.
2. Eat like your great-great-grandmother.
3. Crowd out "food-like products," a.k.a. processed food.
4. Cook more often.
5. Eat mindfully.

Upon reviewing the list, think about what conscious eating practice would have the most impact for you. Identify ONE that you will implement for the duration of the book. If you are not feeling some benefit after two weeks, feel free to modify the practice. Be sure to create a strategy for how you will overcome your barriers for eating consciously.

Finally, listen to the TED Talks and enjoy some of the movies in the additional learning section on our website.

The last word on eating consciously:
**Eat real, whole foods prepared at home
and enjoy mindfully.**

Chapter 7

MOVE OFTEN

When I was in high school my best friend and I had a spare block of time during the day, so we would go to her house and exercise. The purpose was specifically to lose weight. It was hilarious. Sometimes we would do Cher's step workout called "A New Attitude." But we did not have the steps, so we used chairs, which were way too high. Thank God we were only eighteen, because otherwise our backs and knees would have been destroyed.

We would do this specifically with the aim of getting skinnier than we were already. It was fun because we did it together, but I would also force myself to do other workouts, and later, to have gym memberships to get leaner, lose my gut, tone my arms, etc. Never did it cross my mind that there was something more to movement.

As an adult, I expanded my view on exercise to see it as a way to not only stay in shape, but to also enhance my mental and emotional well-being. While physical goals can be very motivating, I learned in my years of yoga training that there was even more to movement than we are taught in our Western society, and it ties in beautifully with being resilient.

I am trained as a yoga teacher and yoga therapist under the lineage of Krishnamacharya. My incredible teachers at Yoga Therapy Toronto studied in Chennai, India, directly with the son of Yogacharya Sri.T Krishnamacharya, who was regarded as the grandfather of modern yoga.

During my years of studies and personal practice, I came to understand the astonishing therapeutic aspects of yoga. Under this lineage, as in other yoga and Eastern traditions, we learn that our bodies have thousands of energy pathways called nadis, or channels. If you have ever been to an acupuncturist's office, you may have seen images or a statue of a human body with these energy meridians depicted. These pathways are a complex system within our bodies where your energy, or to use the yogic term, prana, also known as life force or chi, flows. We were taught that we have 72,000 nadis (channels) moving energy through our system. When the energy is circulating well through the channels, we have health and well-being in all four aspects of our being (physical, mental, emotional, and spiritual). When the energy stops flowing well in a specific area, or there is an obstruction or an energy block, dis-ease can ensue.

Whenever we talked about this, I would picture my parents' pond. Energy, like water, needs to keep moving to stay fresh and alive. To keep the pond clean, my parents have to regularly remove the debris that piles up at the juncture where the water moves in and out to the river. When there is a pileup of leaves, sticks, and dirt, the pond begins to stagnate. So my parents physically remove the debris and move the water around as it exits the pond to prevent it from becoming a dead swamp.

How does this all relate to movement? In short, **we are like water— we need to keep moving and removing energy blocks.** In essence, the movement of our physical bodies causes the movement of energy through all those thousands of nadis (channels). Bodily movement creates an energetic flow within a cohesive pattern that not only makes us stronger, more physically energized, mentally focused, and helps to reduce stress, the energetic flow can also prevent disease, detoxify our bodies, and ultimately lead to health and well-being. So free-flowing prana/energy results in health, while stagnant, blocked, or imbalanced prana flow leads to dis-ease.

As a yoga therapist, I appreciate that yoga is not just a physical practice. It is also a path to reaching your highest potential and ultimately a union with the Highest Source. But this is a lesson on movement, in particular, how it is foundational to our resilience.

Clearly, I am a huge believer in the benefits of yoga through its various gentle stretching asanas (postures) coordinated with breath and (pranayama) breathing exercises. It is an optimal way to move the prana around the body. But, really, other modalities of intentional movement work just as well. It is not the form of movement as much as the function we are looking at.

For those who are not into yoga or energy and need more convincing, in this lesson we will discover the connection between activity levels and cognitive function, happiness, health, and longevity. Basically, I want to provide the scientific evidence behind what a lot of you may know, namely, that movement clears your head, calms you down, helps you focus, and makes you more resilient.

After years of studying yoga, I have it etched in my soul that we are all individual and have Individual Distinctive Constitutional Peculiarities, as my teachers called it. Meaning some of you may have constitutional considerations, health issues, or past injuries that need to be taken into account as you embark on a movement practice. Please seek out help from a health-care practitioner if this is stopping you. Physiotherapy or working with a yoga therapist is a good option to create a customized program just for you.

One of the things I also learned, which is so basic but we, the Western-minded students, all contested is that sometimes if you have an injury, you need a period of complete rest. Rest is critical to healing, but in our culture, we tend to push ourselves even when in pain. Again, we are all individual, as is our path to recovery from an injury, so it may require an individual assessment and treatment plan. But get on it, so that you, too, can enjoy the benefits that come from movement.

Ready? Now onto the goal of this lesson, which is to simply get you moving and to give you tools to stay moving so that you may continue to get stronger, healthier, and more resilient.

So if my yoga energy talk was not sufficient motivation to get you moving, consider what the world's top business leaders and CEOs all have in common. Leaders such as Tim Cook, Sheryl Sandberg, Mark Cuban, and Arianna Huffington all make regular movement part of their daily routine. Unfortunately, the rest of us are not moving our bodies nearly as much. In fact, according to a 2013 Statistics Canada survey, just two in ten adults and one in ten children and youth met the Canadian Physical Activity Guidelines.

What is it these leaders have figured out that the rest of us have not yet discovered? Maybe they have figured out that movement is the "magic pill." We all want something that makes us smarter, happier, and better looking. The good news is that the magic pill exists—and it is movement.

When most of us think about physical activity, we focus on the physical benefits, as I did in my early years: a leaner body, stronger muscles, more flexibility, more coordination. In the later years, perhaps we are motivated by a better heart and cardiovascular system, all encased in a more attractive physique.

More recent research, however, has gone beyond just the physical benefits of exercise and presented compelling evidence of the benefits of exercise on your mind, your well-being, and your mental state. In other words, research has made a direct correlation between physical activity and resilience. Here are some highlights:

Movement makes you smarter. Countless studies have shown that regular physical activity benefits cognitive function leading to improved concentration and mental stamina, increased work productivity and efficiency, sharper memory, enhanced creativity, improved mental state, lower stress, and greater work satisfaction.

In fact, the positive impact of movement on cognitive function exceeds the impact from brain training, drugs, nutritional supplements, and meditation. There is also a large amount of research documenting the significant benefit of long-term, regular exercise on cognition, Alzheimer's risk, and even its progression. More than anything else, exercise is shown to have a positive effect on brain aging and provides resilience to neurodegenerative brain diseases.

How does movement ignite these positive changes in brain health?

Physical activity causes better blood flow and oxygen supply to the brain. This is the main reason you can think better post movement. There is also an endorphin-powered emotional shift that leads to an improvement in focus and productivity.

The benefits of these improvements will spill into your work life. One 2016 study from the University of Southern Denmark studied over 3,500 workers who participated in a workplace exercise program. Upon completion of the program, the researchers saw significant improvements in the health outcomes of participants including a reduction in pain, enhanced cardiorespiratory health, increased muscle strength, and very interestingly, an increase in productivity. The researchers also concluded that the cost of the exercise programs was "acceptable" due to the savings on health expenses and lost productivity. So even though these workers were taking time away from their job to exercise, the organizations they worked for benefited due to their employees' enhanced productivity.

But the work benefits do not stop at productivity. Studies also demonstrate that physically active people who work out during the day also have increased energy, are more creative, less stressed out, and get along better with colleagues. The workplace environment, therefore, improves when employees take some time for movement midday.

Movement makes you happier. Movement burns tension, reduces stress hormones, and activates the happy-brain chemicals known as endorphins.

There are countless studies now proving that exercise makes us not only physically healthier and stronger but happier and more mentally resilient. If you need another study, University of Toronto PhD candidate George Mammen analyzed over twenty-six years' worth of scientific research and coauthored a review that showed that even moderate levels of exercise like twenty to thirty minutes of walking daily can prevent depression in the long term.

Studies have also shown exercise to be an effective treatment for the clinically depressed. In one study published in the *Journal of Biobehavioral Medicine*, researchers assessed the status of 156 adult volunteers with major depressive disorders and assigned them randomly to a treatment program. A third of the participants were treated with aerobic exercise, a third with antidepressants, and a third with both.

After the four-month treatment, patients in all three groups were reassessed and showed significant improvement. The study's initial conclusion was that exercise had an equivalent positive impact on depression as the standard pharmaceutical treatment.

However, after the same group was reassessed six months post program completion, researchers were struck by an amazing finding. What they found was that relapse rates were much lower for those patients in the exercise group. Their conclusion was that exercise has significant therapeutic benefits.

I must share personally while in the depths of my concussion, I was visiting that functional neurologist I spoke of earlier two to three times a week, and he asked me periodically about depression. Despite my head pain, my insomnia, my life, and work being turned upside down, I felt mentally and emotionally okay. I, strangely, did not feel depressed in the least. Both he and his nurses found this to be interesting as they said over 90 percent of their concussion patients struggled with depression. They asked me what I was doing to stay balanced like this. They were surprised it was my daily yoga practice, which filled me with prana, stimulated my vagus nerve, and opened my heart area (which is important, as when we roll in our shoulders and hunch down we actually compress our diaphragm and physiologically contribute to depression and anxiety).

In today's, dare I say, post-pandemic world, where both health-care costs and depression are on the rise, everybody should know about the mountain of research that concludes that moderate levels of exercise, like a twenty-minute daily walk, can ward off depression. Intentional movement also makes us healthier as we discussed already. It increases lifespan, it reduces premature death, it boosts the immune system, and it slows aging. Yay!

A researcher (whom I just adore) named Dan Buettner teamed up with *National Geographic* to find the world's longest-lived people on Earth and study them. They found isolated areas around the world where people statistically lived the longest. What was fascinating about these people was that **they were getting older but were not old**. They called these areas blue zones, and they studied their cultures to find out why.

Through his work, Buettner outlined nine traits that are shared by the longest-lived "young" people on Earth. Number one was "move naturally," which described a way of living that incorporated regular movement like gardening, walking, farming, and household chores.

So if you want to pump iron then have at it, but the benefits from exercise can just as easily come from walking or gardening.

Dr. Roberta De Ra, a chiropractor, who teaches the movement lesson in our online Resilient by Design program, shares a wonderful story illustrating this point. She lived and practiced in Italy for a while, in one of these identified blue zones. She noted that while it was rare to see people out jogging or running marathons, she would constantly see people out walking, biking, carrying groceries, or going for a walk after dinner. She tells the story of an 80-year-old patient who was an avid bike rider. He would go on long bike rides on a regular basis. One day, Roberta complimented him on the fact that he could still ride a bike at his age. And he looked at her with surprise and said, "Well, why wouldn't I? I've been doing it my entire life."

"Do today what you want to be doing tomorrow," Roberta now says. And that is the secret—if you want to be riding your bike, swimming, or even just walking when you are 80, 90, or 100, then start doing it today. Better yet, don't stop doing it in the first place.

So with that, let's dive into the five keys to moving often so that you can build movement into your day in a way that is sustainable and "natural."

KEY 1: Move!

I called this chapter Move Often and NOT Pump Iron or Sweat Often for very good reasons. The key to movement is to look for ways to move yourself outside of the gym.

Consistent, light-impact activity daily is enough to give you all the positive impact of physical activity without ever stepping into a gym. Throughout this section where we discuss exercise or workouts, a brisk walk and some stretching is just as good, and for many of us, it's actually better.

The world's longest-lived people don't pump iron, run marathons, or join gyms; instead, they live in environments that constantly nudge them into moving without thinking about it. You probably don't live in that place, so you DO have to think about it.

The key to movement is figuring out how to be active throughout the day. In our busy lives, the easiest way to build movement in is to move yourself. Walk places, ride a bike, climb up the stairs, do yard work, shovel snow, or rake leaves.

Starting today, begin by looking for alternative ways that allow you to be more active. Move. We all have a natural inclination toward comfort, which is why we circle the parking lot for ten minutes looking for the closest spot rather than just parking a little farther away and walking the five minutes it would take. But too much comfort makes us sluggish. So look for ways to embrace activity. Park farther away and spend that time walking. Your body will thank you for it. Need to pick up the kids from school? Throw on your running shoes and run over to the school rather than drive. Meet a friend for a walk rather than a coffee. These are just a few examples, and they may not work in your life, but the key is to change your mindset to look for ways to engage your body. Walk places, ride a bike, do yard work, shovel snow, or rake leaves—this all counts. **Every little bit of activity helps, and some is always better than none.**

It's surprising how little extra time this takes while still delivering big results. Many of us don't have the ability to set aside a full, continuous hour every day to dedicate to exercise. But most of us can squeeze a few extra minutes here and there. I noticed, for example, that it strangely took me almost the same amount of time to walk the kids to school as it did to drive them. When I would drive, I would often spend a lot of time getting the kids in and out of the car, and even more time finding parking by the school. When we walked or ran because were late, it felt less stressful, and both the kids and I got a mini workout before the start of the day. I also noticed on the days I walked that I always hit my 10,000 steps. The key is to get into the habit of not taking the car or the habit of using those extra minutes to build movement into your day. So take a moment to identify opportunities to move yourself more.

I love this quote that I heard Tony Robbins say in one of his courses: "Sell your car and buy a juicer; the juicer will take you much further."

KEY 2: Make a plan to build exercise into your schedule, preferably at the same time every day, ideally in the morning.

While this seems obvious, it is extremely effective. Planning out when and how you are going to add exercise leads to more of it.

When researchers in one study made people think about how much they planned to exercise, time at the gym increased 138 percent: Spend a bit of time planning and you will end up following through.

I know many of you hear the words "morning workout" and dread the idea. I can sympathize because I was the same. I do not do a workout per se, I do my yoga practice, but I include sun salutations and a series of more active asanas and vinyasas, in the morning.

Starting your day with an active movement practice primes you for excellence according to research.

1. The morning practice/workout enhances your metabolism. Technically, it's called Excess Post-Exercise Oxygen Consumptions or the Afterburn Effect. Basically, it means just that your body continues to burn extra calories even after your workout is over, even when you're sitting at a desk or driving in your car. I love this and find it very motivating, especially on the days I don't want to get out of bed.

2. Morning movement improves your physical and mental energy. It does this in two ways. First, it enhances your body clock or circadian rhythm, which signals your body when to sleep and when to wake up. Exercising in the morning tells your body that it is time to be awake, and it entrains this rhythm. It also optimizes all the functions that the clock is responsible for including improving the quality of your sleep.

Second, not only will you wake up feeling more refreshed, but engaging in morning movement practices is like an all-natural cup of coffee. When you get up and get moving you start to get the blood and energy flowing throughout your entire body. Remember the 72,000 nadis I referred to in the beginning of this chapter? Movement sparks energy to flow through those energy centers. In Western lingo, exercise increases circulation, and you start to wake up your body and prepare your mind for the day, resulting in improved focus and mental abilities. And these benefits stay with us long after we have stopped moving.

3. Finally, the morning movement practice will help you establish the daily habit. Moving first thing in the morning ensures it will happen. When it is scheduled later in the day, other events that seem more pressing may come up and usurp your best intentions. For example, if you plan to exercise in the evening, you run the risk of being exhausted, late from work, feeling overloaded with things to do that must be done, or pulled in a different direction by your kids or family members. I know if I do not do my practice in the morning, no matter what I tell myself, it never seems to happen. First thing in the morning is the time of day when you're least likely to have something "just come up."

Even best laid plans can go awry. So how do we prevent this? First, you make a plan. Then you must consider what is going to stop you from realizing this plan.

If you are like me, it is often the case that I am the one who convinces myself to skip the workout. Plan for this by anticipating your objections and creating solutions. For example, I often tell myself I am too busy, too tired, and that I need more time for family. But I can remind myself that I am better at work, better at problem solving, and more present with my family IF I do my movement practice. So keeping it in my schedule is good for everybody. We all have good excuses, and taking care of our own body seems to get bumped off the list more than anything else. So when making a plan to move, we need to plan for our self-generated roadblocks.

If time is short, then do a ten-minute workout. I find it hard to talk myself out of those. We have included a link to a series of short workouts in the additional learning section on our website.

If I plan to walk somewhere and run out of time, then I ride my bike or park my car partway to my destination and walk the rest.

There is a space between the perfect exercise and no exercise. Preparing for roadblocks and planning ahead allows you to get the movement in your day that you can accommodate.

That is precisely why I love the ten-minute workouts; I cannot make the excuse that I don't have enough time. Honestly, it is just one of those workouts you can do at home. No time spent driving to the gym, changing, showering. Just do it at home. Grab a pair of stretchy pants and go. There is actually a great deal of research now that shows that short intense exercise can induce similar and sometimes superior health benefits to longer moderate-intensity workouts.

KEY 3: Select activities you like, with people you enjoy and music you love.

Planning a walk, yoga, or workout with a friend who likes to move often too will always improve your follow-through.

Anticipating time with a friend makes it fun, like my Cher workout with my BFF. Plus, you made a plan and don't want to let them down. You added some good ole peer pressure to the mix, so you'll never miss it.

As well, research shows music improves exercise performance and reduces your perception of discomfort. So while grit and willpower are great, sometimes the critical factor is that playlist that puts a smile on your face and a spring in your step.

KEY 4: Gamify and keep score of your progress.

When Jerry Seinfeld was asked how he developed the discipline to write every day, he said he made it a game. His advice was to get a big wall calendar that has a whole year on one page and hang it on a noticeable wall. The next step was to get a red marker. He said for each day that he did his task of writing, he put a big red X over that day. "After a few days you'll have a chain. Just keep at it and the chain will grow longer every day. You'll like seeing that chain, especially when you get a few weeks under your belt. Your only job next is to not break the chain."

A simple calendar and a red marker can make all the difference when it comes to being funny—or staying in shape.

For the more tech loving, investing in a wearable fitness tracker or similar technology will achieve the same end. These devices are designed to keep score of your activity levels and gamify the experience of improving activity level. I don't love them, as I don't like to be connected to my phone, and I fear electro-magnetic frequencies blasting me. You can purchase ones now that you can disconnect from your phone.

Either way, there are many wearable fitness devices, and even cellphone apps or similar technology that will track your steps walked, flights climbed, and other movement metrics. These devices are designed to keep score of your activity levels and gamify the experience of improving activity level.

Discover how much movement you normally get and start setting goals for increased movement. The popular suggestion is 10,000 steps a day as a starting point. Apparently, this number does not come from scientific research, but rather from Japanese marketers who were trying to sell a pedometer. Its name translated to "10,000 step meter" in English. Incidentally, the Japanese character for "10,000" roughly resembles a person walking. Ha! Having shared that, Roberta, the chiropractor, shares that it is a worthy goal and that kids from six to twelve years old and post-menopausal women need more than 10,000 a day and should set their target at 12,000 steps daily.

KEY 5: Sit less and stand more.

You may have heard the phrase: "Sitting is the new smoking." The body was not designed to sit for long periods of time. In fact, in a study published by the Mayo Clinic, researchers were astounded to find that individuals who sat for more than eight hours a day with no physical activity had a risk of dying similar to that posed by obesity and smoking. Lifestyles that incorporate high levels of sitting, and specifically prolonged uninterrupted sitting, increase mortality—from any cause.

Sitting for prolonged periods is strongly correlated with increased risks of heart disease, diabetes, cancer, and other conditions. It also results in stiffness. Remember the energy is not flowing through the body when you sit. It is sort of cut off at the hips. People who sit for long periods suffer from increased pain and stiffness in the neck, shoulders, lower back, and hips.

According to the CDC, one in four American adults sits for more than eight hours a day. I actually believe it is more than that, especially in northern countries like Canada where half the year it is cold and dark and people want to decompress by lying on the couch and watching a show after work. British researchers found that office workers sit for up to nine hours a day and that is just in the office.

The real solution to this issue, not surprisingly, is to sit less.

Now I do understand that most of you are sitting right now and have jobs that require you to be in front of a computer. My comments here are going to focus on strategies to reduce sitting in the context of your real life.

Tip number one is to change your workspace to accommodate standing. As I write this, I am reminded to crank up my relatively inexpensive IKEA standing/sitting desk. It's also a mini arm workout! A standing desk is the best way to get you out of your chair position. Fortunately, I am seeing more and more companies adopting sit-stand desks. The *British Medical Journal* published research in October of 2018 stating workers using sit-stand desks demonstrated "improvements in job performance, work engagement, occupational fatigue, daily anxiety, and quality of life."

Tip number two is to have standing or even walking meetings. My boss at the University of Toronto introduced me to this years ago. For our regular weekly business development update meetings, we removed the chairs from the boardroom and had everyone stand. Not only was this a great strategy to get out of our chairs, but it dramatically shortened the meeting time in a positive way. You can even go one step further and have walking meetings. I used to do this with my staff as well. I found it changes up the dynamic, gets people thinking differently, and can be more effective than sitting meetings. I do this on some coaching calls now, where both the client and I walk and talk. It is one way to help get them moving and model this behavior. Having said that, sometimes I have to stop to really listen and be present. Play with it and see what works for you.

Finally, if, despite your best efforts, you find yourself sitting for a prolonged period, remember to stand frequently, ideally every thirty to fifty minutes, stretch, and move around. Set a timer or put meeting reminders in your calendar to get you up.

And when you do get up, don't forget to move your eyes as well! Focusing at close range for long periods can cause eye strain. This often contributes to headaches and loss of concentration. So look away from your computer and give your eyes a rest by following the twenty–twenty–twenty rule. Every twenty minutes, try looking twenty feet away for twenty seconds.

I have included a couple of great stretching videos designed for the office on our website for you to download. They don't require much space or special equipment, and they can be done in most office attire. They are the perfect way to break up a marathon sitting session. Doing these stretches coupled with a short walk is a great way to break up the prolonged sitting sessions.

When you go back into your life and try to implement some of these changes, you will likely discover that corporate culture can be a source of support, as all organizations are waking up to the fact that as our bodies stagnate, so do we. On the other hand, however, it may be the first challenge to overcome. The truth is that most organizations are still full of offices, desks, chairs, and a culture born out of those things. If the organization you work for embraces the goal of getting their people out of their chairs, then the rate of success is usually pretty amazing. If your organization is not one of those, then we have a couple last thoughts on how to be successful.

When others in your office ask why you are standing, keep your WHY in mind as always. Perhaps consider saying something like: "Standing is better for me, it takes the pressure off my back, it breaks up the day, and it helps me stay alert. Adding a couple of hours of standing feels great at the end of the day—you should really try it!"

Now it's time to Do the Work and BE Resilient

Review the Move Often challenge exercise and incorporate the challenge into your life for the remainder of the book.

THE MOVE OFTEN CHALLENGE

Make a decision to move more often.

Review the list of potential activities below and select at least one to implement. Do the activity at least three or four times per week for the duration of the book. If you are not feeling some benefit after two weeks, feel free to modify the practice.

1. Do a ten-minute morning workout.
2. Take a thirty-minute walk in the morning.
3. Take a lunchtime walk.
4. Stretch daily.
5. If you work at a desk, get up and walk around once an hour for five minutes (daily).
6. Use a standing desk for a couple hours each day (Don't have one? Improvise).
7. Walk (partway) home in the evening.
8. Leave the car and walk or bike to complete errands.
9. Go for a run.
10. Go for a bike ride.
11. Take a group exercise class.
12. Complete a ten-minute evening workout.
13. Do any other activity you enjoy that raises your heart rate moderately and gets you moving.

Next, the additional learning section on our website has some great articles and videos in support of the information provided in this lesson, including links to the ten-minute workouts.

As we finish this chapter, I want to bring our focus back to the most important takeaway from this session.

The last word on movement:
Sit less and walk more.
Incorporate movement into every part of your day.

Chapter 8

BREATHE SLOWLY

*Slow breathing is like an anchor in the midst
of an emotional storm: the anchor won't make the storm
go away, but it will hold you steady until it passes.*
–Russ Harris

When I was pregnant with our first daughter, I decided that I wanted to have a natural labor and registered my husband and myself for a "hypnobirthing" course. A couple of my girlfriends had used this technique and had good experiences.

The five-week course took place in a lovely, bohemian yoga studio on a trendy street in Toronto. The teacher was colorful, funky, engaging, and quite bohemian herself. If I recall, she had birthed four kids using the hypnobirthing techniques. The content was fascinating, but to my surprise, it was less about hypnotizing yourself to believe that labor is pain-free and more about learning to put your mind and body into a relaxed state during labor so that fear, muscle tension, and pain subsided. We learned that when in a relaxed, calm state, our bodies produce endorphins that are also natural painkillers.

The key technique was breathing—calm, smooth, long breathing. The instructor explained, "Proper breathing, when wanting to achieve a natural birth, will allow your body to relax and send more oxygen down to your uterus. This way it will be much quicker and easier to birth your baby." Wow, I had never thought about sending oxygen to the uterus and that it would have any impact on the duration or ease of my labor.

We were shown and practiced three different types of breathing techniques. What stuck out for me is they were the opposite of what we see when a woman is depicted in labor on TV. We usually see a panicked woman and partner, breathing out with pursed lips, quickly. Now that I think about it, that kind of breathing is more like hyperventilating. Hyperventilating or rapid breathing can contribute to and exacerbates panic attacks through a vicious circle: fear triggers faster breathing, which triggers greater fear. No wonder in the shows we often see the woman in distress, screaming, and things going awry until a doctor steps in.

This hypno way of breathing was very calming. We were instructed to breathe into our belly for a count of four and exhale for a count of eight. If eight was too long to exhale, you could do six. We could sigh on the exhale as well to release further tension.

Both the pregnant women and their partners in the room practiced this breath in class. We watched women in labor do this breath, but it seemed overly simple to me. We also had some meditations and affirmations to listen to at night that made me feel a bit better about the money we spent.

After the course, I practiced my breathing and listened to my nighttime affirmations daily. And then several months before I was due, my husband ruptured his Achilles tendon while playing squash with a friend. Immediately after the surgery, he had painkillers, but not for the recovery or the physiotherapy. As he had a lot of scar tissue built up preventing him from walking normally, the therapy included having the scar tissue essentially beaten down with a tool that looked like a rubber ball from hell. The ball had spikes on it and was attached to a handle. The procedure was horrible. I once went with Aubrey to his treatment and could not watch the torture. Having watched all these birthing videos in class with me, Aubrey instinctively started to use the hypno breathing techniques. The pain, he said, was so intense, there was no where else to go. As he started to breathe into his upper belly and exhale for longer than he inhaled, something happened—the pain became more manageable, and he calmed and relaxed his body. He felt he could handle it and he did. The physiotherapist said he had the highest pain threshold of anyone he had worked with.

Clearly, there was something to this breathing. Maybe it was a gift. Because of Aubrey's experience, I started to believe in the power of the breath.

I had both my girls naturally using the hypnobirthing techniques. Although my labors were long (thirty-six and thirty-two hours), I was not panicked, I did not scream like an animal as seen on TV or hyperventilate. My babies did not go into distress at any point. My midwives said I looked calm and that I breathed beautifully.

Fast-forward many years. I now have studied and experienced the power of breath or "prana" as it is known in yoga. I may have shared that 99 percent of yoga is breathing.

Breathing, in my opinion and those of the yogis I study from, is the most readily available tool we all have at our constant disposal to reset our nervous system, to become calmer, healthier, and happier. In fact, **I think focused breathing may just be the easiest and quickest way to augment our well-being and resilience.**

Let's dissect the how and why of breathing and its importance in our resilience.

First, a seemingly simplistic question: What is breathing? According to most medical texts, breathing is conventionally defined as the process or action of taking air into and expelling it from the lungs to facilitate respiration (the exchange of oxygen and carbon dioxide).

When you breathe in, your diaphragm contracts and moves downward. This increases the space in your chest cavity, and your lungs can expand into it. As your lungs expand, air is sucked in through your nose or mouth.

When you breathe out, your diaphragm and rib muscles relax, reducing the space in the chest cavity. As the chest cavity decreases, your lungs shrink and the carbon dioxide-infused air flows out of your lungs and out of your nose or mouth.

When we breathe "well," we maximize conditions for health and well-being. Conversely, when the body is tight, stressed, and the diaphragm doesn't move freely, we breathe shallowly, quickly, and "dis-ease" can ensue.

The impact of breathing, therefore, affects more than just our oxygen levels, it can ward off disease by boosting our immune system and lowering blood pressure and cholesterol. Breathing impacts our respiratory, cardiovascular, immune, neurological, muscular, gastro, and cellular systems, as well as our mental, emotional, and physiological well-being. It affects our energy, our sleep, and our whole nervous system by helping us to shift from operating in the sympathetic (stressful fight or flight mode) to the parasympathetic nervous system.

In summary, the way you breathe has an overall effect on the functioning of your whole body and mind. Breathing impacts our entire person, which in yoga is referred to as the five layers of the self or koshas (Annamaya—physical body, Pranamaya—energy body, Manomaya—mental body, Vijnanamaya—wisdom body, and Anandamaya—bliss body).

It is, therefore, no surprise that in the ancient Sanskrit language, breath is referred to as *prana*, the universal life force or primary energy. In yoga, prana is considered the essence of our being. It is the energy that distinguishes the living from the dead.

There is an old Vedic story (the Vedas were India's sacred texts containing spiritual knowledge) where the mind, breath, speech, hearing, and sight argue about which of them was most vital. To settle the dispute, they decided to each leave the body one at a time to ascertain the effect it would have overall. To make a long story short, each left and there was indeed a big impact. When sight left, vision was lost; similarly, when hearing and speech left, the body was shaken and distraught. When the mind left, the person, although still alive, became unconscious. However, when the breath left, the body started to die and with it all the other faculties of sight, hearing, speech, and mind became obsolete as well. They quickly begged the breath to return to the body and announced it was the essence of life itself.

In his book, our yoga teacher from India, Dr. NC, wrote: "The inert physical body is able to perform all its activities only because of prana. Prana enables the eyes to see, ears to hear, nose to smell, hands to grip, legs to walk, and mind to think."

He explained that the physical body is like an electrical instrument and prana like electricity.

The quantity and quality of prana and the way it flows through the "nadis" or energy channels determines one's health and state of mind. Due to our lifestyle, or simply because of the lack of attention we give to our breath in Western society, the energy channels may become partially blocked. When that happens, different ailments can manifest as can stress, anxiety, fear, and other negative emotions.

When the prana level is high and its flow is unencumbered, smooth, and steady, the body is healthy, the mind is calm, positive, and the person is well. Prana, as I learned in my yoga therapist training program, is not only the life force energy, it is also a powerful healing force that can heal the most severe of health issues.

I run a workshop on stress and anxiety. When we discuss prana, most people are not aware that they are not breathing "properly." They are also unaware of the impact of this restricted, shallow breathing on their state of mind and well-being. They do not know that the way you breathe sends a signal to your nervous system. It either says:

"Hey, relax: it's all good, everything is fine, keep all systems functioning" or it shouts: "Alert: danger, speed up the heart rate, enhance our vision, deliver more blood to areas of the body that need more oxygen to get us out of this situation, no time for digestion, run!"

Under extreme stress, I share with the class, people tend to hold their breath entirely. Holding our breath is like oxygen starvation, which is bad in and of itself, but it also further excites the sympathetic or "fight and flight" branch of the nervous system. In other words, you exasperate or reinforce the stress or malaise when you stop breathing or breathe shallowly or quickly.

How do you know if you are breathing well?

It is easier to start with "improper" breath. If you are breathing improperly, you will often feel tension in your back and neck, in your shoulders, and even in your jaw and face. Now this is also a function of the position we take most of the day at the computer, but that is not a coincidence because as we sit at a desk, we constrict our diaphragm from moving naturally. Tight clothes don't help, nor does sucking in our guts.

If we look, we can visibly see chest breathing as opposed to diaphragmatic breathing on ourselves or others. Just look in the mirror. Do your shoulders rise when you breathe in? In chest breathing the diaphragm is prevented from descending. We want to breathe, but we physically cannot. Because we can't breathe in fully, we can't breathe out fully either. So, we may start breathing faster and this leads to mild hyperventilation, which then leads to that cascade of negative emotions stated earlier.

Please test your breathing now:

- Put one hand on your chest and one on your upper abdomen. Breathe in.
- Which hand moves more, the one on your chest or upper abdomen?
- Do your shoulders move up with the inhale? If so, that is chest breathing.

Now let's try diaphragmatic breathing:

- Sit up straight with your feet on the ground or lie down with your knees bent. If you are sitting, roll your shoulders back, relax your face and loosen your jaw, straighten your spine, and breathe in slowly like you are drinking air in through a straw but through your nose into your upper abdomen. Feel your upper abdomen expand. Can you feel your sides and your back expand like an accordion as well? Feel the hand on your belly move up—PAUSE—now contract your lower belly so your stomach moves back in as you exhale through your nose.

- The hand on your chest must remain as still as possible. It will move slightly, but the hand on your belly will move more.

This is diaphragmatic breathing. This is how you want to be breathing. As with learning anything new, the first few times you practice diaphragmatic breathing, it may seem awkward. But did you know this is the way we breathe naturally when we are asleep? While in deep slumber, your belly goes out as you breathe in and then falls. If you have a chance, watch a baby sleep—or anyone, for that matter.

When you aren't breathing consciously, your diaphragm will move downward, but no more than a centimeter. When you breathe consciously, your diaphragm can move downward by up to ten centimeters! That is a huge difference and has a tremendous impact on the amount of prana you take into your body.

This is why the yogis saw breathing practice (pranayama) as more than just breath expansion, they saw it as a powerful means to self-realization. In fact, Richard Rosen describes this process in his book *The Yoga of Breath: A Step-by-Step Guide to Pranayama.*

He says that pranayama is a means of:

- Self-inquiry. By looking at how we breathe, we begin to understand something about who we are.

- Self-transformation. As the yogis say, breath and consciousness are two sides of the same coin. When we change the breath in pranayama, we inevitably change who we are.

- Self-realization. When our small breath becomes one with—and reveals itself as identical to—the Great Breath.

PRANAYAMA AND THREE YOGIC BREATHING PRACTICES

As we have learned, *prana* refers to the universal life force. *Ayama* means to regulate or lengthen, extend either in space or time.

Pranayama is a collection of breathing techniques developed by ancient yogis to control, cultivate, and modify the amount, quality, flow, and direction of prana in the body. Pranayama is often defined simply as "breath control." Pranayama practices involve breathing mostly through the nostrils in a specific pattern of inhalation, breath retention, and exhalation.

Here are a few pranayama practices to try. Please enter with an open mind, try for yourself, and as my teachers say, "See what happens." I have made three videos for you to follow along with me. I find it very useful to be guided by an instructor when learning new practices.

1. The yogic breath is the diaphragmatic breath sometimes referred to as abdominal breathing or belly breathing. We did that earlier. It truly is the foundational practice. Please refer to the earlier instructions or visit our website and try it with me now.

2. Ujjayi breath, pronounced ooo-j-a-ee, is commonly translated from Sanskrit as victorious breath. It is also referred to as ocean-sounding breath. I resonate with the ocean-sounding breath as Ujjayi entails breathing audibly by slightly constricting your glottis (a fancy word my yoga teachers use for the area between the vocal cords at the back of the throat) to create some resistance to the passage of air. The resistance creates an audible "ocean" sound throughout your breath. My teachers always reminded us that Patañjali, in the Yoga Sutra, indicated that breath should be both "dirga" (long) and "suksma" (smooth). Ujjayi is the breath where you can really feel these qualities of breath.

If you have been to a yoga class, it is commonly practiced during asanas (postures), as well as may be practiced when still.

One of the major benefits of Ujjayi is that it helps calm the mind and body. It also helps with being present. You can experience this in particular during a yoga class when you have to maintain this breath with the flow of the class. Add chanting and there is no where else your mind can go. I do the Ujjayi breath throughout the day. For example, I used to reach for my phone while at a red light (a really bad habit), now I just take some of these breaths. Ujjayi also increases the amount of oxygen in the blood, which makes sense to me as it feels like you take in more oxygen during this practice. It also helps to regulate blood pressure. It is energizing and heating, so if you are cool or feeling that midday slump, do a few of these breaths. There are so many benefits, but it's best to try it to see the impact it has on you.

Please try with me now. As you do, please keep in mind that the key to Ujjayi breathing is relaxation; the action of Ujjayi naturally lengthens the breath, which you will recall helps to tap into your parasympathetic (rest and digest) nervous system.

Ready?

- Please sit on a chair or in a cross-legged position on a bolster or cushion. Roll your shoulders back, lengthen your spine, tuck your chin.

- Now inhale through your nose, constricting the back of your throat. Imagine sipping the breath in through a straw. Breathe into your upper abdomen. Hear yourself making that ocean sound.

- As you exhale, you contract your lower abdomen in and breathe out while continuing to make the ocean sound.

- Let's try again by placing your hand on your upper abdomen. When you are ready, breathe in through your nose. Notice how your belly rises and how it deflates on your exhalation. Now, as you inhale, constrict your throat so that you make a sound as you inhale and exhale. When I taught my girls this breath, I called it a "Darth Vader breath." I must have read it described that way somewhere. Anyway, it clicked for them right away, so I'm sharing it with you in case it helps.

- See if you can breathe in for the count of five, pause, and breathe out for five and pause. Do that a few times. Notice if your breath gets longer and if you can breathe in for six and out for six. Do that a few times and again notice what happens with your breath. When you find your comfortable max, see if you can repeat that breath twelve times. After that, breathe in naturally and exhale freely a few times. When complete, observe how you feel.

You can join me online to hear what the Ujjayi breath sounds like and follow along in a mini practice with me.

3. Nadi shodhana. I love actually saying these two Sanskrit words. They are pronounced as one term: *nah-dee-show-dah-nah*. I have spoken of nadis before in the book, they are the network of channels through which energy travels through the body. Shodhana means purification. Therefore, nadi shodhana is primarily aimed at clearing and purifying the subtle channels of the body. Nadi shodhana is commonly referred to as alternate nostril breathing. It is truly one of my favorite pranayama practices because I feel so good after just a few rounds. The studied benefits are plentiful as well. They include, to name a few, purifying the toxins from the nadis (channels), reducing stress and anxiety by calming the nervous system, and infusing the body with oxygen, which all pranayama practices actually do. Nadi shodhana is also known for balancing the left and right side of the brain, and enhancing mental alertness, clarity, and ability to focus. During my acute concussion healing phase, nadi shodhana was my daily go-to for the relief, restore, and reset it gave me. Others depend on nadi shodhana for clearing and balancing respiratory channels. Yet others attest that it restores balance and ease. I see it as a quick and easy resilience-enhancing practice. Please try it with me now.

- Sit comfortably on a chair or on bolster or cushion if you are sitting cross-legged on the floor. The key is you don't want to hunch; you want your spine to be straight. Remember the spine is a highway through which your brain communicates with your whole nervous system and your entire body.

- Take a few abdominal/diaphragmatic breaths. Inhale to your upper abdomen, exhale and contract your lower abdomen. Notice the cool air coming in as you breathe in through both your nostrils, pause, and notice the warm breath as you breathe out. IN–OUT.

- Now inhale through both nostrils. Using the right thumb, close off the right nostril, actually just slightly above the nostril at that bony part. Breathe out through the left nostril slowly and smoothly.

- Pause.

- Keep your right nostril closed and breathe in through the left nostril.

- At the top of our breath, close the left nostril with your ring finger so both nostrils are now closed.

- Pause.

- Open your right nostril and breathe out slowly through the right side.

- Pause.

- Inhale through the right slowly and smoothly.

That is one round of nadi shodhana. To receive full benefits, you want to do twelve or at least six rounds.

Remember even with one nostril closed you still want to be breathing into your upper abdomen and exhaling and contracting your lower abdomen.

You can breathe in to your max and breathe out to your max. Alternatively, you can play with counting your breath. So you can try breathing in for five, holding for five, exhaling for five, and holding for five. If that seems too easy experiment with counts of six, seven, or eight. We were challenged in our yoga program to get up to twenty, although I am staying at a solid ten. You want your breath to be slow, steady, and smooth, so you only move up a count when your breath can keep that steady quality.

The regular practice of deep, slow, smooth breathing exercises can completely change your quality of life and state of mind. Please get familiar with your breath; consider noticing your breath at different points in the day. Then take a few minutes and schedule them in to do some breathing exercises.

In the Yoga Sutras, Patañjali says control the prana and the mind gets controlled automatically. Breathing can still your mind and calm your nervous system. It is your resilience superpower—please explore this unique power you carry within.

Now it's time to Do the Work and BE Resilient

Review the challenge exercise below.

THE BREATHING SLOWLY CHALLENGE

This chapter we learned about three breathing exercises:

1. The Yogic breath
2. The Ujjayi breath
3. Nadi Shodhana

Take some time to decide what breathing exercise you will start with. Choose ONE to begin. Write down when you will do it. First thing in the morning is a perfect time, especially after your morning stretch.

Then commit to yourself that you will do it. It will take you three to five minutes and see what happens. What do you notice? How do you feel? Is there an impact later in the day?

The last word on breathing slowly:

Using your breath, you can immediately reset your nervous system from stressed to relaxed. Breathing is your resilience superpower.

RESILIENCE KEYSTONE II:
SELF-AWARENESS

One can have no smaller or greater mastery
than mastery of oneself.
–Leonardo DaVinci

I once heard the story of a man and his horse. It seems appropriate to start this section with it. You may know it. The story, as many, starts with a peaceful monk walking along a road. Suddenly he hears a galloping horse coming toward him. He stops and turns to see a man riding this horse rapidly in his direction. As the man and horse near, the monk asks, "Where are you going?"

Without stopping, the man on the horse calls out, "I don't know. Ask the horse" and rides away.

Many of us live this way. We are riding quickly in the direction that has been paved by our old habits, programs, and ways of being. We are going so fast we may not even be aware that we are not in control. We may think we are because we're riding the horse.

Now recall as we move into this section that resilience is not this esteemed character trait that a fortunate few individuals possess and others do not. "It involves behaviors, thoughts, and actions that can be learned and developed in anyone," according to the APA.

This is interesting, as in order to cultivate these behaviors, thoughts, and actions, we first must be aware of what we are doing and where that is taking us. We don't want to be like the man on the horse.

Resilient individuals tend to have habits and engage in practices that enhance their self-awareness. But what do we mean by self-awareness?

According to psychologist Daniel Goleman in his book *Emotional Intelligence*, self-awareness is about "knowing one's internal states, preferences, resources, and intuitions."

It is also the ability to monitor our inner world, our thoughts, and emotions as they arise.

To me, this is like having an internal locus of self-control. Someone who is not self-aware is more likely to be a victim to their thoughts, feelings, even their environment. Things happen "to them." Whereas someone who is self-aware is more likely to think "I have power over my thoughts, feelings, and responses." They may also think that "things happen for them." That when a circumstance arises they may not like, it is a growth opportunity.

It is important to recognize that self-awareness is not only about what we notice about ourselves, but also how we notice and respond to our outer world. Therefore, it's no surprise that self-awareness is a key leadership trait. A 2019 study by Cornell University, for example, found that "a high self-awareness score was the strongest predictor of overall success."

In this section, we will explore and challenge ourselves to implement tiny, micro practices that enhance our self-awareness and, in turn, our resilience and overall success in life.

These evidence-based practices include:

- Being mindful
- Generating positivity
- Authentically connecting to others and being discerning about who we connect with
- Recharging and restoring our reserves

Before you dive into the section, in the spirit of neuroscience and building new neuropathways, I want to remind you of some critical success factors:

- Keep your WHY at the forefront. I have mine written out and keep it on my bedside table so I can see it last thing before bed and first thing in the morning.

- Maintain your morning routine. All top performers have morning routines during which they determine what they want to achieve in the day and how they want to show up in the world.

- Do one new thing. For ten weeks, we want you to choose one habit from each lesson to implement and then stack those habits. See what happens when you do.

Chapter 9

BE MINDFUL / BE PRESENT

Mindfulness is not merely a concept or good idea.
It is a way of being. And its synonym, awareness,
is a kind of knowing that is simply bigger than thought.
—JON KABAT-ZINN

I started meditating in high school. I would listen to elaborate meditations, usually with the goal of attaining some spiritually altered state. I had tapes that would guide me through elaborate visualizations. Many of them would be long, and I would do them sporadically, usually when I was not feeling good about myself or wanted to achieve some specific outcome. I had meditations to lose weight, become a confident public speaker, attract abundance, and I even had a meditation to leave my body. I actually really liked that one, as it required me to truly focus and pay attention to the words spoken.

Meditation is often what people think of when they hear the word mindfulness. I was not sure of the distinction between those two terms and where they met.

Mindfulness is actually a funny word. I sort of felt that the word contradicts itself. When I would hear it, I would think of having a mind full: full of thoughts, tangents leading to other thoughts, replays of conversations, old memories, invented memories, ruminations, anxieties of the future, traumas of the past. Essentially, I would think of my own mind, which was abuzz with this constant activity, often disconnected, aimless, and rarely present or at peace.

But that is not mindfulness as you probably already know. The goal of this lesson is, therefore, to explore what mindfulness is and the benefits it offers us. It is also to inspire you to create a habit of being mindful and fully present during specific moments in your day.

WHAT IS MINDFULNESS?

I have taken so many courses on mindfulness, I cannot even count them. Essentially, they all start the same way with a definition of the term followed by a mindful breathing exercise. One class, however, stands out. The teacher, prior to anything else, had us close our eyes. We all sat in a circle and were instructed to hold one hand out. As there was nothing else to do, I listened (a bit apprehensively) to her walking around the room wondering what she was going to do. I could then feel her approach and gently put a tiny round object in my hand. We had to wait until she was done going around the circle delivering everyone this tiny something. Then she instructed us to feel it in our hands. She told us to really focus all our attention and tune into what it was. The process was almost painfully slow. After what seemed like forever, she told us to bring the object to our noses and inhale slowly. I did as she said and was surprisingly flooded with a scent and saliva accumulating in my mouth. She then told us to put the object in our mouth but not to chew it, just to place it in our mouths and notice what arose. I could tell it was a raisin, and my mouth was watering like crazy. It was a plain old, shriveled-up raisin, yet I felt like I could not wait to dig my teeth into it. Finally, she said we could chew it, slowly. In fact, she instructed us to chew it as many times as required to liquefy it before swallowing. I wanted to gobble it up at this point, but I followed directions and I kid you not, that little shriveled-up raisin tasted like a piece of heaven.

During this activity, I experienced mindfulness.

Dr. Jon Kabat-Zinn who is a pioneer in the field of applied mindfulness, describes it as "**paying attention** in a particular way: on purpose, in the present moment and nonjudgmentally."

Notice I highlighted "paying attention." Mindfulness, very simply, is about paying attention. I had, like many of us, trained myself to not pay attention. There are so many distractions in our life: notifications, texts, emails, social media. Being mindful or present is the opposite of skipping around from one thing to the next.

And Kabat-Zinn explains that it is paying attention on purpose. When we practice, we set an intention to direct our attention to the present moment through an object or point of attention.

Your point of attention can be literally anything; it can be sound, breath, bodily sensation, or even a raisin. I not only paid attention to the raisin, but also the process of having it placed in my hand, smelling it, tasting it, chewing it, and swallowing it. I have eaten whole meals and not even noticed, but this one little raisin rocked my world.

Try it with me, and use your body as your point of attention. You can start to scan your body anywhere. Pay attention to any bodily sensations. What are you noticing? What are you feeling? Tune in and stay with it. For me, right now I can feel the keyboard under my fingertips. If I tune into my body, I notice I am actually thirsty. I hadn't realized that. I pause and reach for my mug of green tea with lemon. I raise the mug and inhale. The smell makes my mouth water. I take a slow sip and feel quenched. As I tune in more to my body, I notice my eyes are tired from looking at the screen and my shoulders tense and slightly rolled forward; my one leg is a bit stiff. I stand up, roll my shoulders back, stretch, and take a breath.

Referring back to Kabat-Zinn's definition, mindfulness is also paying attention in the present moment.

Eckhart Tolle, author of *The Power of Now* and many other books that line my shelves, says, "Most people treat the present moment as if it were an obstacle that they need to overcome. Since the present moment is Life itself, it is an insane way to live."

When we are being mindful, we are in the present moment as opposed to in the past or future in a land far, far away. I actually like to refer to mindfulness as presence. I believe being present now with what or who is in front of us actually enables us to have a more impactful presence. In our Certified Resilience Coach Program, I ask our participants, who are executive coaches or people managers, to notice when they are thinking about how they will respond to a client or employee and instead to be fully present with them. I challenge them to make their coaching clients the "objects of their meditation." When they do, they report back that something magical happens. They hear not just the words spoken, but the underlying emotions, they feel when something is not just right, and they get an internal hit or knowing about what to ask next. In some strange way, when you are paying attention, you can expand your intelligence to include not just your thinking brain but also your intuition (or gut or heart).

This leads us to the next part of Kabat-Zinn's definition of mindfulness, which is that it's a practice that is nonjudgmental. I would even say loving or compassionate. Our mind's tendency is to be harsh to ourselves. We are all our worst critics. We will discuss this in the next chapter. Mindfulness invites us to notice ourselves and the world around us nonjudgmentally. Although it is not an easy thing to do, in practice, it means we tune into what is arising, be that bodily sensation or emotion or a thought without getting entangled in it or wishing it were different, whether it is good or bad.

Author Jan Chozen Bays writes in her book *How to Train a Wild Elephant: And Other Adventures in Mindfulness* that "mindfulness unifies our body, heart, and mind, bringing them together in focused attention." She elaborates that "when we are mindful, we are able to engage fully in what we are doing, let go of unhelpful thoughts, and act effectively without being pushed around by our emotions."

So we can notice an emotion such as anger as opposed to being angry. This allows you to step outside yourself in a way. You are not the anger, you are the observer, and as you begin to notice it, something happens. It may be that the anger subsides and you soften or walk away. In most cases, however, it allows you the opportunity to step back and respond vs. react. What is interesting is it enables you to respond with your prefrontal cortex, which you'll recall is your thinking brain as opposed to reacting emotionally with your limbic brain. And this is how resilience develops and shows itself.

Here is a quote by psychiatrist Viktor Frankl that summarizes this beautifully: "Between stimulus and response there is a space. In that space is our power to choose our response. In that response lies our growth and our freedom."

I discovered Viktor Frankl in university. He was a neurologist, psychiatrist, philosopher, writer, and Holocaust survivor. I found his work fascinating, perhaps because my own grandmother and her immediate family spent time in concentration camps as well.

What I believe Frankl was saying here, without ever using the term mindfulness, is that we have the power to choose how we wish to respond to events in our lives, as opposed to reacting to them out of emotional impulses, by noticing and paying attention to the stimulus. In noticing that stimulus, you can also notice your habitual reactions and choose a response that is more in alignment with how you want to be and live. The key is noticing the stimulus; it becomes the object of your attention. This all happens in split seconds, but when you are in the present moment, you can catch it.

A relatable example is being stuck in traffic. The highway you are driving on comes to a halt, and your immediate response may be to get annoyed or even angry. Instead, you notice the stimulus, which, in this case, is the cars around you all braking and slowing down. When you notice the stimulus, you then can wake up out of the autopilot chain of reactions and choose instead how you respond. It may still be with anger, but it may also be with concern for the person who had the accident or gratitude for your safety or for time to practice some mindful breathing.

To finish off this discussion on what mindfulness is, I thought I would share with you this Continuum of Mindfulness created by the Institute of Character. It illustrates for us what mindfulness is by comparing it to what it is not.

MINDFUL	AUTOPILOT/MIND WANDERING
Here, now	Then, later
Skillful responding	Habitual reacting
Aware, present	Monkey mind, distracted
Mode of being	Mode of doing
Allowing/letting be	Fighting the experience
Accepting/facing reality	Avoiding

In looking at this continuum, you can see how being mindful enhances your resilience. In the face of a difficult situation, accepting and facing reality is clearly a better way of coping than fighting the experience or avoiding it all together.

So how do you want to be? Especially if an unexpected adversity strikes?

Dr. Shauna Shapiro states: "What we practice grows stronger."

We have an opportunity now to be aware of what we are practicing and choose, like Viktor Frankl said, how we want to be. Are we practicing being stressed all the time, distracted, unable to focus, restless, unsettled, and habitually reacting and fighting? We can instead choose the now, choose to be present and aware of ourselves and those around us, and as we do that more and more, the neuropathways of being mindful will get stronger and stronger.

BENEFITS OF MINDFULNESS

Before we jump into some mindfulness practices for you, I wanted to share, in case you need more convincing, that there has been an explosion of research into mindfulness and its benefits to our emotional, mental, and physical health and well-being.

EMOTIONAL REGULATION

Research shows that those who engage in regular mindfulness practices have decreased reactivity in stressful situations, heightened response flexibility, and enhanced affect and emotion regulation, as well as decreased rumination.

This beautifully ties in with being resilient. Recall that being resilient is like having shock absorbers, so when something unexpected happens, you feel more steady. Mindfulness, according to the research, is shown to basically develop those shock absorbers by enhancing our ability to regulate and respond vs. react to unexpected adversity. New research into the Covid pandemic, for example, shows that those who engaged in a mindfulness meditation practice regularly reported higher levels of emotional well-being, improved mood, and reduced symptoms of anxiety and depression during the lockdowns.

Mindfulness has also been shown to make us happier. According to researcher Gilbert Killingsworth, when our minds wander, we tend to be less happy. Killingsworth, who studies attention, also found that our minds wander about 50 percent of the time. He called the article, "A wandering mind is an unhappy mind."

STRESS REDUCTION

Mindfulness also seems to reduce perceived stress and builds an inner strength so that future stressors have less impact. That sure sounds like resilience to me. I participated in the Mindfulness-Based Stress Reduction (MBSR) Program created by Jon Kabat-Zinn. We learned that stress and anxiety arise when we feel that the challenges facing us are unsurmountable. The stress hormone cortisol is released by the hypothalamus in the brain when a stressful situation occurs. Mindfulness research showed that cortisol production decreases significantly in the brains of subjects who participate in a mindfulness program such as the MBSR. Stress hormone levels were found to remain low, hours after the meditation sessions had ended. The amazing thing is that the impact of stress reduction does not just translate to feeling better emotionally and mentally, it also improves sleep, lowers blood pressure, and improves healing and health.

PHYSICAL HEALTH

This leads me to the physical health benefits of mindfulness, which are incredible. Mindfulness practice can maintain a healthy heart, and practicing mindfulness can improve blood circulation and lower heart rate levels. There are lots of studies on how practicing mindfulness contributes to a stronger immune system, enhanced quality of sleep, improved pain tolerance, and decreased perception of pain.

What I find amazing and particularly relevant to me is that during the height of my concussion, which also happened to be the height of Covid lockdowns, I became increasingly aware of the impact of mindfulness meditation on brain health and healing. First of all, while pain meds, acupuncture, chiropractic sessions, and even my beloved yoga could not help me, meditation could. A particularly beneficial meditation practice I used was yoga nidra, a form of yogic sleep that puts you in a hypnagogic state.

MRI and fMRI (functional MRI) imaging are now being used to observe changes to the structure and function of the brain. We can now actually observe the impacts of a mindfulness meditation practice on the brain. The prefrontal cortex, the seat of executive function otherwise known as the thinking brain, is thickened, and the amygdala, that superhero that wants to protect us from danger but can be way too over-reactive, is diminished with mindfulness practice.

Based on studies with aging populations, scientists now believe that a consistent mindfulness practice can help bolster brain function and decelerate memory loss. When we pay attention and are present to what is now, it seems that miracles can happen.

FIVE PRACTICES TO BECOME MORE MINDFUL

As we finally dive into some mindfulness practices to practice, I wanted to give credit to Michele Milan, President of Centre for Mindful Leadership, who worked with me on these. Michele is also that amazing boss I referred to earlier on. She teaches in our online Resilient by Design program, and so I have incorporated her work and words here along with mine. More information about Michele can be found in the Resources section.

MINDFUL PRACTICE 1: Formal practice

This first mindfulness practice is what we would refer to as formal practice or meditation. Recall at the beginning, I did not know where mindfulness and meditation met. Now I do. Mindfulness is the formal meditation practice.

Generally, when people think of mindfulness practice, they think of meditation. Meditation is not the only mindfulness practice, but it is a core practice, and it is where we will begin. You don't need any fancy cushions or yogic positions. You can even do this in your chair at your desk. It is generally best to take a relaxed but alert position.

If you are seated in a chair it is helpful to have the spine upright but not rigid. Take a dignified position, as we say in yoga. Your feet flat on the floor, and your hands folded on your lap or resting on your thighs if that is accessible to you.

Many people prefer to close their eyes, but it's also possible to have a soft focus with eyes downcast. The practice itself is very simple.

We choose our focus or point of attention. Often, we begin with the breath because we all have it. Then we focus our attention on the object of choice. Eventually, we become aware that our attention has wandered. And we gently escort it back to our focus. Then we repeat. Again, and again.

That's it.

But that moment of noticing our attention has wandered is key. There can be a tendency to see that as a moment of failure and then judgment begins. You may think, "I'm terrible at this. I just can't do it."

That same teacher I had the raisin experience with drew this image, which has helped me with this immensely.

She shared, in this example, that your point of attention is the line in the middle. Your mind wanders off, but you notice it and gently bring it back to center. It wanders off again in another direction, then you notice again and bring it back. She used the analogy of downhill skiing; you ski out, but you come back to the center, and so on. As you become a better skier, you come back in faster and stay closer to the line.

The key is not that your mind wandered, it is that you noticed it and brought it back. In fact, it's an exercise in what is called meta-attention, or attention to attention, and is an opportunity to develop the muscle of paying attention, acceptance, and self-kindness.

It is actually an essential part of practice.

Let's try a short, guided mindful breathing practice. This practice comes from Michele Milan, President of Centre for Mindful Leadership.

To begin, you may assume a dignified and comfortable position. If you're in a chair, it is helpful to move your back away from the back of the chair and to place your feet flat on the floor.

Gently close your eyes, if that's okay for you.

Now, notice any physical sensations in the body.

Bring into awareness the sensations present in your body at this time.

Sensations of the body supported by the chair, the feet on the floor, perhaps clothing against the skin. Whatever is present for you.

Notice where there is relaxation, where there is tension.

Notice if bringing these sensations into awareness changes them in any way.

Now allow into awareness the sensations of the body breathing.

There is no need for you to do anything special or to change anything, the body knows how to breathe. Just note sensations of breathing wherever they are most vivid for you in this moment. This may be at the nostrils or the back of the throat. It may be the expansion and contraction of the rib cage or the movement of the chest or belly.

Just allow into awareness the nurturing, easy flow of the breath as it moves the body.

Your breath, just as you find it today.

This is the intention of this practice.

Breathing naturally without effort.

Resting in the breath, in the effortless breath.

If you find you are thinking about the experience, about whether you are doing it correctly, just let that go, accept, and gently guide your attention back to the breath itself with kindness and with ease. If it helps you may label thoughts as thinking.

Then let them go.

There is no right way or wrong way. There is only your experience in this moment. There is nowhere to go and nothing to do.

See if you can be present with curiosity.

Follow this breath now through the length of the inhalation, and notice the turning point, where inhalation becomes exhalation.

Follow this breath now through the length of the exhalation and another turning point, aware of this breath with openness and curiosity.

Different, perhaps, than the one before it.

And this breath now, also different.

(Silence)

If your attention has wandered, escort it back again.

If you notice challenging sensations arising, just note them, and bring curiosity to them.

If you feel the need to change position, do so gently with intention and then come back to the focus of this practice, which is on the sensations of breathing wherever they are most vivid for you.

Not doing. With no effort. Just breathing.

The whole body breathing naturally.

However that feels.

Whole body breathing without effort.

(Silence)

Awareness and acceptance of the breath, just allowing the breath to be as it is. Being with it just as it is, in this moment.

Being with your experience just as it is, in this moment.

And finally letting that go.

Expanding awareness again to the whole body breathing.

Whole body sitting.

Here.

In this moment.

Whole body.

In this moment.

Now.

And when you are ready, opening your eyes and bringing this practice to a close.

(Pause)

So if you just read that, you have not really experienced a mindful breath meditation. I suggest you take this script and record yourself reading these words slowly. Then play it and follow along. It should not take more than three minutes. Once you do the practice, take a moment to observe how you feel. What do you notice?

Incorporating a mindfulness meditation practice into your day is simple, does not need to take a lot of time, and will most definitely strengthen your resilience.

You can practice in silence with just a timer, or you can use guided meditations available through apps or online. I have included links to a few short practices on our website for you.

MINDFUL PRACTICE 2: Informal practices

Informal practices are those that can be attached to other activities and integrated into your day. Because mindfulness is a way of being, we can use everything we do as an opportunity to practice. Because I cook so often, I now use chopping vegetables as an informal practice. I am totally present as I chop those carrots. When my mind wanders, I keep coming back to them.

Examples of informal practices include:

Diaphragmatic breathing: If you notice you are tense, stressed, or anxious, try taking a few slow and deep diaphragmatic breaths as we did in the breathing chapter. Inhale to the count of four to your upper abdomen—pause—exhale and contract your lower abdomen to the count of four and hold for four. If that doesn't feel right, just inhale into your upper abdomen, then exhale and contract your lower abdomen. Repeat a few times. Recall that controlled breathing, especially when your exhale is a bit longer than your inhale, triggers the parasympathetic nervous system or the relaxation response.

Mindful eating: Try eating mindfully or even in total silence as we discussed in the Eat Consciously chapter. Set yourself up for success by removing distractions, i.e., put away your phone, tablet, and shut off your television. Focus your attention on your food. When your mind wanders away from your food, bring it back over and over again to the smell of your food, the texture, the taste. Chew super slowly, and remember to put your fork down between bites. Don't stop there. Why not be totally present with your dish washing? Ruminating about your day or thinking of what you will do after you finish cleaning is not being present with what is. "Wash the dishes to wash the dishes," my teachers said.

Mindful walking: Here is a new one for you to try. I first discovered mindful walking at a silent retreat I attended. We walked barefoot on the lawn. It was early morning and there was dew on the grass. It was cold and wet and the sensation on my feet was strong enough to hold my attention. Walking is so familiar and ordinary, we often fail to even notice it. Recall mindfulness is paying attention in the present moment. We rarely pay attention to walking unless it generates some sort of pain. So next time you aren't in a rush, pay attention to the sensations of the body as you walk. How do your feet feel on the ground? Notice where you put your weight first and then what happens. What happens as you move one foot in front of the other? Do you feel a change in balance? Notice what muscles are working? Are your arms swinging at all as you walk? Walk fully aware of your body for a bit. Then expand your awareness to your surroundings. What do you see around you? Do you hear anything? Notice if you can hear any birds singing? What about any smells?

Mindful walking is so simple and all you need is you, your body, and your attention.

Mindful showering: Showering is the perfect time to practice mindfulness. You are alone, quiet, and undistracted for a period of time daily. After being introduced to the practice at a mindfulness workshop first created at Google called *Search Inside Yourself*, I noticed that while showering, my mind generally wandered. In other words, I was not present; in fact, I seemed to be in autopilot. In contrast, the mindful showering practice invites us to "wake up" and be fully present. It is actually a very sensual experience in that we are to be fully aware of and focused on our physical senses. I like to start my mindful shower before I actually get in the water. While I wait for the water to warm up, I tune into my breathing and take a few slow, deep diaphragmatic breaths. I notice the sound of the water and notice if heat or steam start to fill the room. Continue as you step in the shower, notice the temperature change, in particular the sensation of the water on your skin. Go through your usual routine but perhaps a bit more slowly, paying attention to sensations, and bringing your mind back every time it wanders off, again and again. As you finish your shower, see if you can stay fully present while drying off and as you commence the rest of the day.

Use triggers

A mindfulness trigger is something that reminds you to break out of "autopilot" so that you can be present, mindful, calm, and free of the ruminating mind. A trigger can help you build a new habit. Recall that when stressed or distracted we revert to old habits, so it is nice to have tools that help us remember our "new way to be." Mindfulness triggers can be anything: an action you do daily or an object in your environment. For example, I make a smoothie daily. It blends for eighty-five seconds. That is time for me to take almost six full deep breaths. I do the same with the kettle. While it boils, instead of running off, I stay there and breathe. Here are some other ideas to play with:

Thích Nhat Hanh, the Buddist teacher, suggested posting little notes around your house and/or office to remind yourself to smile and relax.

When your phone rings, do not answer right away. Take one to three slow deep breaths to release what you're doing and remind yourself you have a choice to be present and friendly with whoever is calling.

Michele teaches her clients to take three slow breaths when sitting down to work in the morning. The goal is to fully arrive and be present and focused with your work.

Entering a room is a great trigger. For example, bring attention to your hand touching the door handle before you walk through the door to a team meeting. Pause and take a breath. Remind yourself how you want to show up. You may even visualize sending light to the people you are meeting with. To transition from work life to family time, you can do the same. You can even associate a phrase with the trigger. For example, as you open the front door you could say, "I leave work behind and open my heart." Then smile.

MINDFUL PRACTICE 3: Mindful pauses

I hope you are seeing that being mindful or even engaging in more formal mediation practices need not take a lot of time. In fact, micro-meditations, and informal mindful practices as I have presented, are gaining a lot of traction in peer-reviewed research.

I recently stumbled upon VIA institute's practice of the Mindful Pause. I found it to be simple, short, and quite beautiful. It is also a great resilience-enhancing tool for challenging situations. For example, before you go into a difficult meeting or conversation, this practice can help you release some stress, focus, and perhaps most importantly, remember you have powerful strengths to call upon.

This Mindful Pause is very simple; it has only two steps. This is part of why I like it so much.

- Step 1: Stop what you are doing. Lengthen your spine, bring attention to your body, and PAUSE. While you pause, feel your in-breath and out-breath for ten to fifteen seconds. I actually set a timer for a minute.

- Step 2: Conclude with a question: Which of my character strengths will I bring forward right now?

A character strength can be any quality. A few examples include: love, gratitude, nonjudgment, emotional intelligence, empathy, playfulness, leadership, curiosity, and, of course, listening. Which brings us to the next mindful practice.

MINDFULNESS PRACTICE 4: Mindful listening

Our final practice is one that may come in handy in meetings or maybe with your partner, child, parent, or friend. I was introduced to this practice while participating in an eight-week mindfulness-based stress reduction program. It was one of my favorite practices. I am not naturally inclined to mindful listening. In my family, we, much to my husband's surprise, have a habit of not only finishing each other's sentences, but of interrupting. In fact, if you want to get in on the conversation, you must jump in and interrupt someone or you may never be able to speak. I say this half-jokingly, but needless to say, I had a lot to learn in the area of mindful listening. As an aside, my husband is now a great interrupter.

Mindful listening is really the opposite of the way I learned to engage in conversation. It is a way of being totally present with someone and giving your full attention to what they are saying. One way to look at it is the person speaking is your object of meditation. You are paying attention in the moment to them in a nonjudgmental way. Recall that is the definition of mindfulness. Just as in meditation, the key to mindful listening is to simply notice when your mind wanders off, and then to bring your focus back again and again to center, which here is the person speaking.

It is listening to understand, instead of listening to reply or get heard. It is listening without comparing, constructing stories, without needing to solve the speaker's issue, or even advise them. There is no agenda. It is just listening.

In the mindfulness program, we had to take turns speaking and listening. The first time we did this face-to-face, the second time back-to-back. After each time we listened, we had to recount what we heard. I found I could almost recall verbatim what my dyad partner told me in the back-to-back exercise. I was totally focused and not only heard her words but actually felt her emotions. When I shared what I heard her say, using her words, she got teary-eyed and said she hadn't felt heard like this by anyone in years. It is a powerful practice to use both at home and work. Try it and see what happens.

Here are some best practices for mindful listening:

- **Be fully present.** Do not multitask. It is ineffective anyway, and the person knows if you are half listening to them while reading your emails or scrolling on your phone. If you cannot give someone your attention, consider whether it might be better to postpone the conversation until you can be fully present. You might even consider shutting off notifications on your device. I have heard that certain organizations are now asking staff to put their phones in a designated tray so they will pay attention during meetings. Can you believe it? We are so addicted to our devices we have become like children.

- **Be intentional.** Set the intention to focus your attention on the person with whom you're speaking. I have to do this with my children more. When I set the intention to be fully present, I find our talks are so much deeper and more heartfelt. Like in meditation, if your mind wanders from what the person is saying, notice and bring it back to the sound of their voice, their words, their tone. If you've missed something, it is okay to ask for clarification. Asking for clarification is not disrespectful; it actually shows that you want to understand them.

- **Hear between the words.** Notice not only the words spoken, but the full range of information coming your way. What is the facial expression, tone of voice, and body language of the person speaking? What can you feel, and what is the speaker feeling?

- **Use your breath not your words.** Breathe in and out slowly.

Remember, where your breath goes, so goes your mind. Stay focused on the speaker's words and resist the urge to interrupt. Also, resist the urge to offer advice and to share your own experiences. I often want to interrupt and say, "Oh my God, me too" and go into my similar experience. That is not to say you can never do that, but during a mindful, important conversation, pay attention to the speaker fully until they are finished. In other words, stay quiet until they are done speaking, then take a breath and respond kindly. You may even, like in the mindfulness program I completed, reflect back what you heard them say.

Listening in this way allows you to pick up on more of what is actually going on in the conversation. You will notice that people notice if you listen to them mindfully. Your connection with others generally heightens, as does your empathy.

MINDFULNESS PRACTICE 5: Silence

Our world is so loud these days. From the moment we wake up to the time we go to bed there are constant distractions around us that take our attention away from ourselves. I would argue there is a cacophony of noise from music and morning shows on the radio while we drive, to the news on the TV while we get ready, then there are the YouTube reels, interesting podcasts, Netflix, Spotify, not to mention people around us. This is not all bad, but I definitely noticed at the height of my concussion that constant background noise adds up and impacts not only our nervous system, but also our very presence.

Silence is the antidote to this hullabaloo of external noise. I see it as a needed counterbalance. The good news is that you don't need anything to engage in this practice. You just need to set a time to shut out all the noise and be. I like to do this at least a couple of times a week when I walk our dog. I do not take my phone, as I may be tempted to call someone or listen to a podcast. I set an intention to be mindful in my silence. This is an important step. I may walk mindfully and then take some time to really listen to the sounds around me. I am always amazed when I do this how loud the birds sing.

Another practice is to set a timer for say ten minutes to engage in a mindful meditation. Just be in the silence; notice the silence. When your mind wanders off, like in all the other practices, bring it back gently again and again.

A final silence practice that you may consider is one I learned about in the book *In the Sphere of Silence* by Vijay Eswaran. The practice is to be done in solitude first thing upon waking. He suggests devoting an hour for this, but I did it for forty minutes, as I also wanted to do my yoga and breathing.

For the practice you need a journal and pen as well as a self-development book.

The practice is as follows: You dedicate your first thirty minutes to writing about your long-term and short-term goals. You write them out each day, then take some time to analyze your progress and what you need to focus on today.

Next, you take twenty minutes to learn. You pull out your

self-development book and focus on it for the allotted time. The author suggests reading mindfully for ten minutes, and then writing a summary by hand for ten minutes to integrate the learning.

Finally, you put your timer on for ten minutes and do a silent mindful meditation.

The challenge is to try this practice for twenty-one days in a row and observe what transpires in your life.

Just becoming aware of silence is good. When I'm in the car, I often turn off the radio and just drive. When I cook, I used to always want to listen to something; now, I intentionally cook in silence a few times a week. It is truly a mini resilience reset.

Now it's time to Do the Work and BE Resilient

As I write this, I want to share that I think this whole book is about mindfulness. We are becoming increasingly mindful of how we treat our bodies and spirits as we augment our resilience. But for the purpose of the challenge exercise, we will focus on the mindfulness practices presented in this chapter. Please review them and choose one practice to implement for the remainder of the book.

THE MINDFULNESS CHALLENGE

Please choose ONE practice to implement.

1. Formal practice
2. Informal practice
   - Diaphramtic breathing
   - Mindful eating
   - Mindful walking
   - Mindful showering
3. Mindful pause
4. Mindful listening
5. Silence

Consider when you will do your chosen practice daily.

Also consider attaching it to a trigger to make it easier.

It may seem like we've covered a huge topic, but really, this is just the beginning because mindfulness simply must be experienced; it must be practiced. The real journey of mindfulness is not one that occurs in lessons or books. It occurs in you, in the now moment while doing the practice.

The last word on mindfulness:

Being mindful can make you not only more resilient but also happier. It is foundational, and it is possible—with practice.

Chapter 10

GENERATE POSITIVITY

You cannot have a positive life and negative mind.
–Joyce Meyer

I recently worked with a client, a lovely retired woman, who had lost her husband prior to Covid. She was very fearful, watched the news regularly, did not see her kids or grandkids for fear of catching the virus and dying, and did not go out in the world unless to a doctor's appointment. Not surprisingly, she was depressed. Her sister suggested some yoga therapy with me via Zoom, and because we could do it online, she agreed.

Our first session, her energy felt heavy. She was clearly down and struggling. She was quite surprised, however, when in addition to some breathing exercises and gentle prana opening movements, I assigned her to watch stand-up comedy. She said she didn't like it, as often the comedians were rude. I gently challenged her to do some research and find one or two she liked. I told her to go on Netflix and watch as many as she could until she found one who really made her laugh. In addition, she was to avoid watching the news.

She contested. I assured her that if something big were to happen in the world, she would quickly be informed by friends and family. We agreed to meet the following week at the same time.

When I jumped online for our second session, even I was surprised by the woman I met on the other side of the screen. She was entirely different. She sat differently: spine straight, not hunched like the week before. She had a sparkle in her eye. Her energy was light and playful, and she definitely did not look down or depressed. She immediately started our call with a huge smile and the statement: "I did my homework."

She then shared how so many of the stand-up comedians made her giggle, but there was one in particular who she could not stop watching. He made her laugh so hard that she actually checked out his website to learn when he was coming to town. WHAT? This was a lady who never left her home, not even to buy some bread. Although she was not ready to go to a stadium yet, she did note that she felt less fearful in general and was perhaps ready to see family. Nothing had changed in the external world. But she had changed as she chose to focus on joy, and her fear was releasing a hold on her. What perplexed her was that in addition to feeling happier, she also noted that she slept better that week, and as a result had more energy and physically felt better. It was like a positive feedback loop.

Our following sessions continued to build on this practice of generating positive emotion and of being mindful of triggers that brought her down. She realized that to generate positive emotion she had to first be aware of her emotions and what precipitated them.

And here is where resilience comes in: this lovely lady, through building the habit of generating positive emotion with daily and consistent mindful practice, was able to handle tough, even scary, situations with more ease. Our last session together was the week of a heart procedure she needed to have. It was essentially heart surgery. What amazed me was how peaceful and positive she was about the procedure. She reframed it as a way to heal her broken heart and be whole and happy again. Not surprisingly, when I heard from her post surgery, she was recovering quicker than the doctors had anticipated.

This lovely client had laughed (and breathed) her way to resilience, and I dare say, life became easier and more fun for her.

Research shows that resilient individuals tend to have a positive mindset. In this chapter, we will focus on how to generate this positive affect to further build our resilience. My goal here is also for you to become aware that you have the power, much like my client did, to determine your emotional state, and that doing so is a key to more ease in life and resilience.

I think you will agree with me that the quality of your life is largely determined by the quality of the mental states you live in day to day—states like love, anger, happiness, fear, and excitement. Strangely, what happens in your life does not necessarily determine how you feel. How you feel is the result of how you use your own mind to interpret the situation. Recall my client who reframed her heart surgery to be about "mending her broken heart" and being able to fully love again. Suddenly she was not a victim of her heart not working properly; instead, she chose to see it as an opportunity to love again unabashedly.

This whole concept really turned my world around. I, like many, tended to attribute my emotional state to what was happening in my external environment: I succeeded or failed at school or work; I was promoted or recognized for my hard work; I was financially doing well or not so well; something good happened or something bad occurred. Good or bad, pleasure or pain—my emotions were like a game of ping-pong, and as a result, I was happy or sad, down on myself or feeling great. And further, it wasn't my fault how I felt, it was a result of the outside world.

Many of us live in this place of constantly being pulled in one direction or another by things or conditions we either want or hope to avoid, and the fatalism of this perspective can be comforting because then our sad moods can be blamed on something external.

But then comes yoga to shake us up. My yoga teachers encouraged us to cultivate equanimity, upeksha in Sanskrit. It is a way of being, a virtue in Buddhism actually, that is very the opposite of the emotional ping-ponging I described earlier. Upeksha refers to the quality of being calm, especially in the midst of difficult situations. It is a psychological stability and composure that is not depressed or elated by external happenings. One of my teachers used the example of being on a rocky boat and all the people on the boat running to one side when the boat rocked that way and then running to the other side when it rocked the other way. The equanimous individual stands in the middle of the boat. They are balanced, centered, and have an inner calm despite the surrounding chaos.

My teachers taught that we are constantly being pulled in one direction or another by things or conditions we either want or hope to avoid. This is the ego, they said, and its craving for pleasure and position. It does not lead to happiness, well-being, or resilience. So how do we stand calmly in the middle of the rocking boat? We have to notice the moment when our emotions feel intense and take a deep breath. In her book *Comfortable with Uncertainty*, Tibetan Kagyu teacher Pema Chödrön said, "To cultivate equanimity, we practice catching ourselves when we feel attraction or aversion before it hardens into grasping or negativity."

Said another way, we need to be mindful and self-aware. Notice that Chödrön said we do this before the "attraction or aversion hardens into negativity." I interpret that to mean that staying centered and positive is directly connected with paying attention in the present moment to our thoughts, feelings, state of mind, and even our body as it speaks to us as well.

For those who are not yogis and need more convincing, as I shared earlier, I worked in the field of executive education for about ten years, and now in my business, I deliver workshops to leaders and executive coaches who work with leaders. Interestingly, the calm, centered, equanimous way of being and a positive outlook are key leadership traits. They enable leaders to overcome obstacles and set a positive tone in the workplace. A positive, equanimous attitude can neutralize chaos and disruption and allow a leader to course correct through any negativity. Employees feed off the attitude of these leaders during times of uncertainty. Said in another way, those leaders and the organizations they work for are more resilient. Positive workplaces are directly correlated to high levels of engagement among the workforce. Positive workplaces are also directly correlated with higher levels of loyalty. Higher loyalty translates into lower turnover, which means lower corporate memory loss, more job progression, and reduced hiring costs.

And if you are an employer, that's all good for business. It's also why organizations are so interested in building resilient leaders, teams, and organizations. In studies by the Queens School of Business and by the Gallup Organization, they calculated the impact of a disengaged workforce on business and found that disengaged workers had 37 percent higher absenteeism and 49 percent more accidents. And as a result, organizations with low engagement scores had 18 percent lower productivity and 16 percent lower profits.

POSITIVE PSYCHOLOGY

For the answer as to why steady positive emotions contribute to enhanced resilience, and performance in general, we have to look to the relatively new field of positive psychology. Psychologist Martin Selgman, who is known as the father of positive psychology, describes positive psychology as "the scientific study of optimal human function that aims to discover and promote the factors that allow individuals and communities to thrive."

Prior to this positive psychology movement, mainstream psychology was primarily concerned with what is wrong with us. Who falls below the average level of happiness, or struggles with sadness, anxiety, stress, or depression and how to elevate them to "normal" (that dreaded word). At the time, the profession of psychology was not focused on why certain people performed significantly better than others and how that might enable the population to thrive.

This began to change in the early 2000s when the leaders in the field acknowledged that they were only looking at half of the equation. Since then, there has been an explosion of research and work done to explore the factors that contribute to a positive psyche and the benefits of this state.

An example of this work is the Happiness Advantage, a term coined by author and Harvard professor Shawn Achor. Achor's TED Talk "The happy secret to better work" is so funny. Honestly, I have now watched it many times, and it always makes me laugh out loud. The short talk is also very informative and clearly resonates with people, as it has over 25 million views. Achor says the following about his research: "We're finding it is not necessarily the reality that shapes us, but the lens through which your brain views the world that shapes your reality."

BOOM! He goes on to state that **"Ninety percent of your long-term happiness is predicted not by the external world but by the way your brain processes the world."**

Achor and other positive psychologists state that feeling positive causes your intelligence, creativity, and even your energy to rise. Recall my client who noticed her sleep and energy improved when she started listening to comedians instead of news anchors.

So, it seems all good things in life, including performance at work, are aligned with positive emotions. I would even argue that longevity itself is correlated with the ability to generate positivity. Here is a study I find fascinating, introduced to me by Professor Julie McCarthy at the University of Toronto. The study was conducted on the Sisters of Notre Dame in Milwaukee. There were 180 nuns, living in one convent. They were all around the same age and had the same living conditions. As part of the study, the sisters were asked to write an account of their lives at the convent. Based on the account written, each nun was assigned to one of two groups: group one were those expressing positive emotions and group two were those who tended toward the negative. Now this experiment was neat for the researchers, as a lot of the external factors that usually get in the way of studies and bias results were eliminated. The lives and routines of these nuns were exactly the same. They lived in the same conditions, ate the same foods, and none of the sisters smoked, drank alcohol, or took drugs, as these were forbidden and frankly not available. The nuns were all unmarried, and none had children. They had the same economic and social status and had the same access to health care. Interestingly, there was a wide range in how long they each lived, which naturally one could attribute to genetics. However, more interestingly was that the amount of positivity the nuns expressed in their life stories seemed to be directly correlated with how long the nuns lived.

Here is the data from the study. The researchers found that:

- 95 percent of the most cheerful quarter, but only 34 percent of the least cheerful quarter, were alive at age 85.
- 54 percent of the most cheerful quarter, but only 11 percent of the least cheerful quarter, were alive at age 94.

Researchers looked for other factors that would contribute to the longer lives. They started with how devout the nuns were, how well written the life accounts were (perhaps indicating a distinct level of education), they even looked at how much they looked forward to the future. None of these factors seem to have a correlation to their life span. The only factor seems to be the amount of positive feeling expressed in their life story. The researchers therefore concluded: "A happy nun is a long-lived nun."

So the nuns' research flies in the face of the old happiness formula that we alluded to earlier. Let's call it the "I'll be happy when" model that told us that happiness was correlated to achieving or getting something in the external world. I'll be happy when I graduate, when I am promoted, when I find the love of my life, when I have a family or fancy new car or house—and the list goes on.

This way of thinking causes us to be stuck on the hamster wheel of unhappiness. But before you blame yourself, we need to acknowledge that in many ways, this is the model of happiness we are taught by society (in the West anyway) by our schools and parents and reinforced throughout life. Current research into positive psychology shows that this model is scientifically broken and backward.

When we achieve our goals, we do have a short-lived boost in happiness. But then it fades, and we set new goals or just move the old ones out a bit further and begin the grind again. If you get the job, then you want the next job. If you complete your sales targets, you then create higher targets, and so on and so on. What we end up doing is creating a reward system where the goal of long-term happiness is perpetually around the corner.

What this model has us doing is making sacrifices in terms of living happily today in exchange for the promise of BIGGER happiness tomorrow. The problem is that the happy tomorrow never comes—we have to find happy now in the moment.

Are you convinced to choose joy now? Well, how do we do that?

The answer is almost silly. **The way to become more positive is to generate more positive emotions.**

Unlike early psychology, the modern version teaches that positivity or happiness is generated from within us. Regardless of our lot in life, we can choose how we respond to our environment. Do you enjoy the life you have and the moments that make up that life or are you focused on the future or worse, what is lacking or deficient? When you fail, do you declare yourself a failure or do you view failure as teacher on the road to accomplishment? Reframing setbacks and adversity are key to resilience.

There is a great quote by Mary Engelbreit that perfectly captures this resilient way of being. She says, "If you don't like something, change it; if you can't change it, change the way you think about it."

One of my favorite authors, Wayne Dyer, has a similar quote: "When you change the way you look at things, the things you look at change."

There is a quantum component to this quote that I won't get into now as I am not a quantum physicist, but truly something changes when you decide to change your perspective from an emotional victim to a mindful chooser of emotions. Again, we are back at mindfulness and that moment of pause after a stimulus occurs, when we can choose happiness.

As the revered monk Thích Nhat Hanh said, "There is no way to happiness—happiness is the way."

FIVE PRACTICES TO GENERATE POSITIVE EMOTIONS

You and I can CHOOSE to be happy and generate positive emotions from within. The following are five practices to help you to foster a more positive way of being, even if your life is not "perfect yet."

POSITIVITY PRACTICE 1: Ritualize gratitude

What I mean by that is to create a practice of gratitude in your life so much so that it becomes a new habit or way of being wired in that beautiful limbic brain of yours.

Being grateful is not just saying thank you. It is the act of intentionally noticing and appreciating the good in your life, however small or big. Gratitude changes your perspective on the world and your life when you shift your focus from what's not working to noticing what is. Noticing your friends, family, health, success, joy, the sun, a flower, or even a smile from a stranger can enhance your mood almost immediately. Gratitude, according to positivepsychology.com, can be both a trait as in a character strength and a state of being. As a character strength, you actively seek out things to be grateful for. As state of being, you feel the positive emotion from the act of taking in and appreciating the good.

The key to note is that gratitude is a resilience-enhancing practice in and of itself. Researchers have found it to be positively correlated with social, emotional, and psychological well-being. Dr. Rick Hanson states, "Gratitude, gladness, and related feelings like appreciation are easy to dismiss, but studies in fact show that cultivating them has lasting and important benefits, including lifting your mood, increasing satisfaction with life, and building resilience."

The sad thing is that often, we are inclined to focus on the negative and to keep score of the bad experiences. Recall Dr. Hanson's analogy that "the mind is like Velcro for negative experiences, but Teflon for the positive ones."

Our brain, to help us survive, developed this negativity bias, which means it naturally prefers looking for, recreating, and storing negative experiences or information over the positive ones. What a gratitude ritual can do is help you to circumvent this reptilian survival instinct. When you express gratitude for the good things in your life, however tiny, you shift your attention toward the goodness. You start to notice and feel what is good, you relive it, and you start to scan for more of it. Remember: what you practice grows stronger, and similarly, what you focus on, you find more of.

Ritualizing gratitude can take many forms. A very common practice championed by Oprah in the '90s is the gratitude journal. Keeping a gratitude journal teaches your subconscious to consistently look for things to be thankful for. It is important to do this every day, especially on bad days. I once heard of a story of a mother who was struggling with her teenage daughter and decided to take five minutes each night to not only note but also feel something good about her daughter. Not only did her relationship with her daughter start to improve, but at the end of an entire year of compiling these good things, she gifted her daughter this journal. Imagine how loved and appreciated this teenage girl felt.

Consider keeping a journal beside your bed. Each evening write down two or three things that you are grateful for. Heck, even one is good. Make the items recent and specific and include enough detail to not only make them real for you but to elicit the emotion. When you do so, you are flooded with good-feeling chemicals. "Experiencing gratitude activates neurotransmitters like dopamine, which we associate with pleasure, and serotonin, which regulates our mood. It also causes the brain to release oxytocin, a hormone which induces feelings like trust and generosity, which promotes social bonding, and feeling connected," states Amy E. Keller, PsyD and Licensed Marriage and Family Therapist.

It is also a fun activity to do with kids at dinner or at bedtime. Our girls love to go around the table and share our highlight of the day.

There are countless ways to practice gratitude. It doesn't matter what you do, just that you do it.

POSITIVITY PRACTICE 2: Cultivate kindness

Whereas gratitude often results when people receive kindness from others, kindness entails enacting kind behavior toward other people. Have you ever noticed it is more fun to give a present than receive one? My girls caught onto this a while ago and always fight for the present they made or bought to be opened first.

Our brains love kindness. Did you know that our neurological reward systems show similar activity when we win money as when that same amount is given to a charity of our choice? Researchers at the University of British Columbia tested this theory by giving away money. Half the people in their study had to spend it on themselves and the other half were required to spend it on others. Each research participant was interviewed at the end of the study, and they found that people given $50 to spend it on others were actually happier than the participants who spent the money on themselves.

We all know how to be kind. We just need to get kindness back on our radar so we can choose it. The reality is that in this hectic, fast-paced world too many people operate head down, headphones on, trying to stay above water, and get through the day. Living this way, kindness may have fallen to the wayside.

No act of kindness, no matter how small, is ever wasted.
–Aesop

So we are going to retrain ourselves to be kind and feel its benefits through random acts of kindness. Within the challenge exercise, you are going to be performing random acts of kindness daily. Here are some ideas of where you can start. Notice how simple they are.

- Help an elderly neighbor do some chores.
- When you go for a coffee, pick one up for a work colleague too.
- Say something nice to a complete stranger.
- Let someone cut in line at the grocery store.
- Refrain from road rage. Send love to the person who cut you off.
- Hold a door open for someone.
- Volunteer at a soup kitchen.
- Send a funny YouTube video to someone.

- Help a person cross the street or carry their groceries. I still fondly remember a young boy in France who grabbed my heavy groceries and ran them over to the bus for me. He recognized me from our regular bus route.
- Smile!

(For more ideas be sure to check out: randomactsofkindness.org)

POSITIVITY PRACTICE 3: Engage in self-compassion

Having self-compassion means being able to relate to yourself in a way that's gentle, forgiving, kind, accepting, and loving. It is rooted in Buddhist psychology but more recently championed by Dr. Kristin Neff. She divides the practice into three components.

1. Self-kindness. Rather than being critical when we fail at something, treat ourselves with love and empathy.

2. Common humanity. Rather than judging ourselves for our personal flaws and challenging experiences, see them as part of a broader human experience.

3. Mindfulness. Rather than avoiding or over-identifying with a difficult situation, maintain a non-biased awareness of the experience, even when it is painful.

What is important to note is that self-compassion is distinct from the practices of gratitude and kindness in that it does not necessarily generate good feelings in the moment. Dr. Neff explains, "Self-compassion is a practice of goodwill, not good feelings . . . With self-compassion, we mindfully accept that the moment is painful, and embrace ourselves with kindness and care in response, remembering that imperfection is part of the shared human experience."

I have struggled with self-criticism and perfectionism my whole life. I have followed the work of Tara Brach on *Radical Acceptance* and *Radical Compassion* as well as gobbled up Brené Brown's books, including *The Gifts of Imperfection*. In this process, I discovered that a lot of self-criticism and perfectionism stems from seeking external validation and is based upon deep-seated feelings of unworthiness. The practice of self-compassion is an antidote to those. It is a way to circumvent these feelings and behaviors to find peace and "good enoughness" as Brown says. My practice, because I have children and love them unconditionally, is to see myself as one of my children. It sounds funny that I see myself as my own child; however, when I notice myself going down the dark path of self-deprecating thoughts, I like to step outside of me, see myself as the 7-year-old with pigtails I once was, and send her love.

If you want others to be happy, practice compassion.
If you want to be happy, practice compassion.
—THE DALAI LAMA

This quote brings us to a neat tool for practicing self-compassion.

The exercise is to think about a time when a close friend felt bad about themselves or was really struggling in some way. How did you respond to your friend in this situation, assuming you were centered and at your best? Write down what you did or said and note the tone in which you typically talk to your friends.

Now think about times when you feel bad about yourself or are struggling. How do you typically respond to yourself in these situations? Write down what you typically do, what you say, and note the tone in which you talk to yourself.

Did you notice a difference? If so, ask yourself why. What factors or fears come into play that lead you to treat yourself and others so differently?

Please write down how you think things might change if you responded to yourself when you're suffering in the same way you typically respond to a close friend in their time of need.

Why not try treating yourself like a good friend and see what happens?

For those who need assistance generating their self-compassion, especially the emotions that go along with it, another great practice is the Loving Kindness Meditation (LKM). I still remember the day I was first introduced to this meditation at a silent retreat. It opened my heart like a newborn baby would, and I actually cried. The LKM, for those who aren't aware, is a guided meditative practice that focuses on several key principles, among them compassion for self and compassion for others. It is a method to relieve suffering through the sending of kindness and love. It is a practice that opens us up to the idea that people, including ourselves, deserve a feeling of well-being, safety, and love.

The meditation apps we have suggested have many versions of the LKM on them for you to try.

POSITIVITY PRACTICE 4: Identify your strengths

Identifying and focusing on your strengths (as opposed to focusing on your weaknesses) will raise your level of joy as well.

Martin Seligman, whom I've mentioned before, says that for a person to be truly happy and live a meaningful life, they must recognize their personal strengths and use these strengths for the greater good. It is like the Japanese concept of "Ikigai." Ikigai, according to Ken Mogi, author of *Awakening Your Ikigai*, is an ancient and widespread concept for the Japanese, which translates simply to "a reason to get up in the morning" or, more poetically, "waking up to joy."

Ikigai has usually been referred to as *both* a personal pursuit of happiness and one that is of benefit to others through self-mastery.

Dan Buettner, author of the Blue Zones whom I referred to in the Move Often chapter, claims that Ikigai not only contributes to self-satisfaction but also longevity. He insists that people with a strong sense of Ikigai live up to eight years longer. Buettner, therefore, suggests making three lists: your values, things you like to do, and things you are good at. The cross section of the three lists is your Ikigai.

Notice again the importance of knowing and focusing on the things you are good at, i.e., your strengths. Strengths tend to be things we are good at, enjoy doing, and that are beneficial to others. There are many online "Find your Ikagai" worksheets to guide you through the process of finding the intersection of your strengths, values, and their meaning in the world.

Alternatively, consider just making a list of your strengths, and instead of focusing on identifying and improving your weaknesses, concentrate on what you are great at. I know this may not be realistic, but I would argue we tend to swing more in the direction of noting our weaknesses, so this type of exercise is a welcome counterbalance.

Research shows that employees who can use their strengths each day are up to SIX times more engaged in their work. Imagine that! Gallup analysis also shows that those employees are three times more likely to report an excellent quality of life and are 8 percent more productive than employees unable to use their strengths and are less likely to quit their jobs. If you are an employer, you definitely want your staff zeroing in on their strengths.

The problem for many of us is that we don't know what our strengths are. We can list our weaknesses, but articulating our strengths is not as easy.

Here is an activity you can do. Think of a story about you at your best and write it out in detail. What did you do, how did it impact upon you and others, what was the outcome of the story? Write out all the details and share it with your accountability partner. Discuss with them what strengths you hear coming out of the story.

In addition, like with almost everything else in the world, there is also an online tool for finding your strengths. The Clifton Strengths Assessment is a great online tool to help explore your strengths, although there is a fee for this service. There are multiple other assessments you can play with. This is the one we have used with organizations as it is quite comprehensive.

POSITIVITY PRACTICE 5: Laugh

Yes, I want you, like my client, to crowd out the news, scary, sad movies and TV shows, and submerge yourself in stand-up comedy. Do this for one or two weeks and see what happens.

According to researchers quoted in the *Journal of Hospital Medicine*, children laugh about 400 times per day, whereas adults about 15 times. In *The Joy Diet*, Martha Beck challenges us to laugh at least 100 times per day.

Not only that, studies have shown that laughter is good for our health. It relaxes the whole constitution, relieves stress, decreases stress hormones, and triggers the release of endorphins that make you feel good and even relieve pain. It boosts the immune system, is good for your heart, and in a word, makes you resilient.

Dr. Lee Berk of Loma Linda University Medical Center, California, has been conducting laughter therapy research since the late 1970s. A one point, Berk decided to study the effects of laughter on ten healthy male subjects. Five of them had to watch an hour-long comedy while the other five didn't. Berk then had all ten subjects take blood samples. The results were not difficult to interpret. Cortisol (the hormone our body releases under stress) decreased more rapidly in the comedy-watching participants. Berk's experiment indicated that the level of natural killer cells (a type of immune cell that attacks virus and tumor cells) increased in the subjects who laughed for an hour. These same cells are suppressed if the body suffers from consistent stress.

On top of all that, laughter just simply feels good. We need no studies to prove that we feel lighter when we laugh. The ability to change our focus, even perspective in hard situations, is what makes laughter such a simple yet powerful resilience-enhancing tool. It is no surprise that Mark Twain said, "The human race has one really effective weapon, and that is laughter."

So, the challenge is to laugh as much as you can. Stand-up comedians are a good place to start; funny movies work too. Tell jokes, have your kids tell you jokes, and remember, no news!

Now it's time to Do the Work and BE Resilient

Feelings are a great motivator and learning to generate positivity is all about feeling joyous emotions. Consider how raising your positivity level will improve your life, your relationships with coworkers, friends, family, and even your productivity.

Now make the decision to be more positive and put into action ONE of the positivity practices for the remainder of the book. At a minimum, set a goal to maintain your practice for two weeks and then *see what happens.*

THE GENERATE POSITIVITY CHALLENGE

1. **Ritualize gratitude.** Notice and appreciate the good. A good practice is starting a daily gratitude journal.

2. **Cultivate kindness.** Engage in daily random acts of kindness. Hold that door open for the person behind you and smile; let someone in when you are stuck in traffic; help someone elderly.

3. **Engage in self-compassion.** Be gentle and kind with yourself, especially if you make a mistake. Try a Loving Kindness Meditation.

4. **Identify your strengths.** Know and focus on things you are good at. Consider discovering your Ikagai, the intersection of your strengths and purpose.

5. **Laugh!** Like my client, embark on a journey of finding what makes you laugh and then determine how you will ramp up your full-bellied laughter every day.

Take a moment now to choose to be positive despite the external circumstances. Your practice will help you.

The last word on generating positivity:

You have the power to generate positive emotions despite external circumstances. These feel-good emotions not only make you happier, healthier, and more resilient, but they can also lengthen your life.

Chapter 11

CONNECT AUTHENTICALLY (AND WITH DISCERNMENT)

Connection is why we're here;
it is what gives purpose and meaning to our lives.
–BRENÉ BROWN

"Z jakim przystajesz takim się stajesz." My mom used to repeat this Polish proverb to me and my siblings. It translates to something like the person you stand with, such a person you become. It doesn't have quite the same ring in English, but the essence is something like you become like the person you hang out with. I think an English equivalent is "Who keeps company with the wolves, will learn to howl." So be very mindful of the company you keep.

Look at those around you, and if they are howling—i.e., are super negative, angry, and always complaining—run! You will not only be drained by their howling, but they will rub off on you. Dr. Christiane Northrup has a great book on this called *Dodging Energy Vampires*. This is not just theory, it is supported by neuroscientists in their findings on mirror neurons and how essentially our brains, via these mirror neurons, mimic the behaviors they see. More on this later.

My lifelong BFF often tells the story of how her mom, who was our Polish Girl Scout leader, put us together for all activities, as she felt I would be a good friend for and influence on her daughter. Clearly, she was a Polish mom living by the "one you hang out with, you become" adage. I am flattered and blessed that she picked me as the friend, as not only did we become besties in elementary and high school, we went onto university together, traveled a big chunk of the world together, and now our families are entangled, and our husbands have no choice but to hang out and get along.

I share all this, not as a nice fuzzy friend story but because this is where resilience comes in. My friend and I have literally pulled each other up off the floor from broken hearts, broken dreams, feelings of doubt and insecurity, fear, loss, and sometimes from a little too much tequila. We have been each other's cheerleaders and big-dream holders. Our friendship has been a shock absorber for the bumpy roads. It not only made the ride across the bumps of life smoother, it sometimes even turned the bumpy ride into a fun adventure.

What you will discover in this lesson is that resilient individuals have a handful of these solid, deep, authentic, and positive relationships. As the American Psychological Association wrote in its resilience report: "Many studies show that the primary factor in resilience is having caring and supportive relationships within and outside the family. Relationships that create love and trust, provide role models, and offer encouragement and reassurance help bolster a person's resilience."

So the goal of this chapter is to understand the critical value of real human connection in dealing with adversity or achieving success and to explore five ways to perhaps improve the quality of our connections.

Let us begin with the definition of connection. To do so we turn to dear, revered Brené Brown. For those who don't know Brené Brown, she is a professor at the University of Houston who has spent more than twenty years studying courage, vulnerability, shame, and empathy. She shows up in a way that you want to connect with her, at times vulnerably and most always authentically. She defines connection this way: **"Connection is the energy that exists between people when they feel seen, heard, and valued. When they can give and receive without judgment and when they derive sustenance and strength from the relationship."**

I love that she starts the definition with the idea that connection is an energy exchange, and where there is connection, people derive strength, a.k.a. resilience.

Ironically, when Covid hit, and we needed connection the most and the resulting resilience it provides, we were told to self-isolate, social distance, and quarantine away from our loved ones to prevent the spread of the virus. I think that took more of a toll on many of us than the virus itself.

A study published in the journal *Brain, Behavior, and Immunity* found that loneliness was the strongest predictor for post-traumatic stress disorder, depression, and anxiety. Connection is, therefore, of utmost importance now because we have seen this huge spike in isolation. And Covid aside, our modern, Western society has been struggling with loneliness. In fact, the most common type of household is now a single-person household, and almost 30 percent of Canadians live alone, which is the highest it has ever been.

Not only does connection help us navigate the ups and downs of life better, psychologists and medical researchers have long ago proven that authentic, loving connections and a solid community positively impact our physical, mental, and emotional well-being.

Julianne Holt-Lunstad, a psychology professor at Brigham Young University, analyzed data from 148 studies involving more than 300,000 people. She found that people with social connections had a 50 percent lower risk of dying early compared to people who did not have strong social ties. That's remarkable—a 50 percent lower risk of dying early if you have strong connections.

Additionally, Dr. Emma Seppala, a Yale professor, author, and speaker, found links between strong social connections and physical, mental, and emotional well-being. She indicates that having solid social connections "leads to a 50 percent increased chance of longevity, strengthens your immune system, and helps you recover from disease faster." Wow! This clearly suggests that social isolation was not a good strategy for Covid spread prevention.

In fact, researchers at Harvard University put forward that having no friends could be as deadly as smoking. They made this attestation after they discovered a tie between loneliness and the levels of a blood-clotting protein that can cause heart attacks and stroke.

To arrive at this conclusion, these Harvard researchers compared levels of the blood-clotting protein with the numbers of people a patient had in their social circle. They were surprised to find a correlation. As the number of social connections fell, the level of the blood-clotting fibrinogen rose.

Connected people are also less likely to be depressed, as I alluded to earlier.

Anyone who has experienced loneliness (which is probably most of us) will intuitively understand the research findings that prove those who are more connected experience lower rates of depression and anxiety.

Dr. Seppala's research found that those who feel connected to others "have higher self-esteem, are more empathetic to others, more trusting and cooperative, and as a consequence, others are more open to trusting and cooperating with them." She also highlights that this creates a positive feedback loop wherein connected people feel cheerful and chatty—and this cheerfulness helps them attract and connect to other cheerful people.

Researchers have also found that if you feel you belong within a social group, chances are you will be happier and more satisfied with life. The findings show that identifying as part of a group gives people a stronger sense of purpose and security, as well as providing support when times are tough.

Researchers at Nottingham Trent University studied almost 4,000 individuals and looked at how much each person identified with their family, local community, or a group of their choice, such as a sports team or a hobby group. The research team then measured each participant's level of happiness using detailed questionnaires. They identified a clear correlation between feeling connected to a group and happiness. Moreover, they identified the more connected the study participants were to their community or social groups, the higher their levels of well-being.

A strong support network can also lead to greater success in life. It makes sense that strong connections provide support when challenges arise and enable greater levels of risk-taking. A great example I read is that of trapeze fliers. Trapeze fliers, although very skilled at their art, know that sometimes seconds will not align with their partner or the bar they reach for. They are able to take daring risks to entertain us because they know there is safety net in place that will catch them if they fall. Strong social connections are like that safety net. They allow us to jump and stretch knowing if something goes wrong, we are supported.

Think about this for a second in a typical work setting. If you like and respect the people you work with and they like and respect you, and you know that they will dig in and help you if required and cheer you on when you win and won't try to tear you down if you fail, you're going to be more willing to take on big challenges.

It is quite self-evident that we as social animals need others to thrive and survive. With that I want to move on to five ways to be more authentically connected to the people you resonate with.

FIVE KEYS TO ENHANCING AUTHENTIC CONNECTIONS IN YOUR LIFE

The following are five ways to improve the quality and, perhaps, the quantity of your connections. I know that some of this will seem obvious, and it is. I also know that some of you do this more naturally than others. As further motivation, please consider this quote from Julie Suttie: "How resilient we are may have as much to do with our social milieu and circle of support as it does with our personal strengths."

1: Set an intention to enhance your connections

With relationships, we tend to take a passive stance. Unlike movement, sleep, eating, or even mindfulness, we may assume that we are not in control. We don't choose the people around us like we choose to eat a salad instead of a hamburger. We didn't choose our parents or siblings as far as our consciousness knows, and we don't usually choose our work colleagues. The first key asks us to rethink our passivity and realize we are not victims of our relationships or lack thereof.

Take a moment now to assess the connections in your life. Perhaps make a list of your closest family members and friends. Ask yourself:

- Do you feel socially fulfilled by this person?
- Do you feel good around this person? You may drop into your gut as you think of them.
- Do you feel accepted, uplifted, and at peace with them?
- Do you have similar values and views on key issues?
- Do you laugh a lot with this person?

Now, we cannot expect another to make us happy, and generally people treat us as we treat ourselves. But these are good indicators of how positive your relationships are. It goes without saying that when in doubt, lean out. What I mean by that is consider leaning out of relationships that drain you and bring you down. Life is too short for energy vampires, as Dr. Northrup attests.

Now with this insight, set an intention. It may be to limit your time with people who lower your vibe and give more of your time to those who make you giggle and smile. Consider doing this without guilt or shame. Your intention may also be to attract a new soul family.

My intention at the moment is to attract more like-minded, joyous souls to my life and also to attract a feeling of community.

What is your intention?

With intentions, we have to write them out and then imagine them as done or act as if they were already true. But that is not enough. We also have to make the effort. Brené Brown says, "Courage starts with showing up and letting ourselves be seen."

So, once you set the intention, make the effort to first actually show up. Then when you do, be authentic.

We are all so busy and often set in our ways due to existing habits etched in our limbic brain. We need to bushwhack new neural pathways of being social, putting ourselves out there, and being a new person who is not too busy for friendship and fun.

2: Be fully present with others

The second way to improve your connections is to be mindful and present when in the presence of others. Dale Carnegie, in his book *How to Win Friends and Influence People*, writes: **"You can make more friends in two months by becoming interested in other people than you can in two years by trying to get other people interested in you."**

As I mentioned earlier, I often tell the coaches in our Certified Resilience Coach Program to make their client the object of their meditation. What I mean by that is to really pay attention and focus on the client, in the present moment and nonjudgmentally.

Did you notice that was the definition of mindfulness?

When your mind wanders away from the person, gently bring it back to the person, to their voice, to their words, over and over again. Being fully present with the other also means to listen, absorb, and understand before speaking. Recall the mindful listening practice. As I shared, this did not come naturally to me.

We all want to be heard and understood, and because of that, we tend to focus on how much of the speaking time we can get. As a result, many of us don't fully listen to others when they speak. We have all caught ourselves in a conversation of not listening but rather figuring out what we are going to say. This results in a conversation looking more like a duel. It also leaves us without the benefit of what the other person was trying to share, not to mention a lost opportunity at real communication and connection.

The best way to avoid this is to first focus on listening and understanding the other person. Don't think about what you are going to say, don't think about your opinion of what they are saying, focus on truly paying attention in the moment and understanding their point of view. Ask questions of a clarifying nature. Get into who they are and what they think.

A perfect practice for this section is to notice if you are ever being a phubber. What is a phubber, you ask? For those of you who don't know this term, I want to assure you that we have all been the culprits and the victims of this act. The proper term is "phubbing," and it is a word used to describe the habit of ignoring someone in favor of your phone. I have noticed myself looking at my phone while being on a Zoom call or webinar. I am really embarrassed to admit it, but it is true. Our mind cannot do two things at once, so ultimately, we are neglecting the speaker and, in a way, telling them they don't matter. Not a good way to make friends, as Carnegie would say.

If you really want to connect and you want the other person to know that you genuinely want to connect, put your phone away and make them your point of focus.

3: Be mindful of your words and don't gossip

Again, my dear mom's voice comes to mind as I start this section. She would (like many wise moms) say, "If you have nothing good to say, don't say it."

Smart, but not easy to do, especially when our ego is involved. I recall reading the book *The Four Agreements* by Don Miguel Ruiz. It is a book based on the wisdom teaching of the Toltecs, who were an ancient, Indigenous people of Mexico. In the book, he explains that we are brought up by society in ways that tend to hurt us, and he offers this new set of "four agreements" to use in life. The first agreement is to "be impeccable with our word." Ruiz explains that words are extremely powerful. He states that our "word" (as in the Bible, "In the beginning was the Word") is like a force that we create with. We can create good or bad thoughts, emotions, and outcomes. Our words are so powerful that he says they can even "cast black magic" on the people we say them to. This flies in the face of the saying "Sticks and stones can break my bones, but words will never hurt me." Well-meaning adults would say "Don't listen to them," but kids know how painful words can be. I must admit some of the hurtful words that bullies spewed upon me still ring in my ears at unexpected times. It's like they are etched in my subconscious.

So, a key to connection is to be mindful of our words, as they can cut. That goes for gossip as well, Ruiz points out. I hate to admit it, but gossiping can be fun and even feel like bonding with the person you are gossiping with, but inevitably you are making yourself feel good by talking, usually negatively, about another.

Rumi, the sage thirteenth-century poet and scholar, wisely said, "Before you speak. Let your words pass through three gates: Is it true? Is it necessary? Is it kind?"

4: Namaste your connections

Most of us know this scene: at the end of a yoga class, the teacher, sitting cross-legged, presses their palms together in a prayer gesture at the chest, inhales deeply, and bows down chanting, "Namaste." Do you know what Namaste actually means? It's not just a respectful farewell. *Nama* means bow; *as* means I; and *te* means you—Namaste means "I bow to you." My yoga teachers explained that we bow down with respect to each other as we are all Divine or have the sacred within us, we just don't realize it. By seeing the Divine or love and light in the other, you are not only humbled and see them as their highest self, you enable them to become their best self. You also start to transform the way you interact with them. And as my teachers always say, "Do this, and something will happen."

Namaste asks us to look past the three-dimensional human in front of us: their appearance, status, success, or failure, and instead see that love and light.

Wayne Dyer tells this story of Baba Muktanada, who was considered to be one of the greatest saints born in India:

"Baba, what do you see when you look at me?"

Baba said, "I see the light in you."

The person replied, "How can that be, Baba? I am an angry person. I am terrible. You must see all that."

Baba said, "No, I see the light."

Consider seeing the Divine or Light in others this week and see what happens.

5: Choose who you connect with discernment

We come full circle to the Polish proverb to be mindful of who we spend time with. You may have heard it presented by motivational speaker and Tony Robbins's teacher, Jim Rohn: "You are the average of the five people you spend the most time with."

Our energy, our positivity, and our level of commitment can all be affected, for better or worse, by the people we connect with the most. Not convinced?

According to neuroscientists, we all have "mirror neurons" in our brains that mirror or mimic what they "see." A good example we can all relate to is being in a group of people where one person starts to yawn. Generally, and uncontrollably, we start to yawn. It is mirror neurons in action. Italian scientists discovered these mirror neurons when observing that when one monkey picked up a banana, another monkey observing the banana being picked up had similar brain activity. In other words, the same parts of the monkey's brain lit up whether the monkey physically picked up the banana or was just watching another monkey picking up the banana. Interesting.

The researchers noted that mirror neurons are essentially "empathy neurons." They allow us to see and feel what the other is going through. Apparently, even hearing someone speak positively or seeing someone smile helps you to feel better. And as we know from our neuroscience lesson, what you practice grows stronger; so if you surround yourself with happy, healthy, and wise people, you will practice being happier, healthier, and wiser. And over time, that is who you will be!

By choosing who you spend time with, you are choosing sincerity or cynicism, positivity or negativity, high energy or low energy, social engagement or selfishness.

Choose wisely!

Now it's time to Do the Work and BE Resilient

We have a fundamental need for human connection. This connection can positively impact on our physical and mental well-being and can be a source of power and resilience.

THE CONNECT AUTHENTICALLY (AND WITH DISCERNMENT) CHALLENGE

Please review the five practices to augment your connections. Which one do you resonate with most at the moment? Choose that one to implement for the remainder of the book or at least two weeks. Here are the practices for you:

1. Simply set an intention to enhance your positive connections and do it!

2. Be fully present with others. Remember no phubbing.

3. Be mindful of your words and don't gossip.

4. Namaste your connections: see the Divine and Light in others.

5. Choose you who connect with discernment. If your connections are negative, lean away. Watch your vibe and that of the people you surround yourself with.

The last word on connecting authentically
(and with discernment):

Healthy relationships help you not only overcome difficulties but also to thrive!

Chapter 12

REST AND RECHARGE

*Almost everything will work again if you unplug it
for a few minutes, including you.*
–ANNE LAMOTT

At a loss of what to do or be when I "grew up," I went to do an
International MBA (IMBA) after finishing my Bachelor of Arts
degree. I had not touched calculus, statistics, economics, or finance
since high school. To make things worse, the IMBA program was
bilingual, delivered both in French and English. While my French,
at the time, was decent enough to pass the oral interview with the
program directors, it was nowhere close to being fluent. As someone
who graduated at the top of my class in high school and was on
the Dean's Honors in my undergrad, I was not only determined to
pass the courses, but the type A perfectionist in me pushed me to
strive to be at the top of the class. Well, if anyone has done an MBA,
they know that the program, though not difficult from a content
perspective, is super heavy in terms of workload, and has unrealistic
expectations, deadlines, and artificial time pressures the whole year

through. In fact, we used to say it felt like trying to take a sip of water from a fire hydrant. We were simply bombarded with work.

Thank God I was in my early twenties and did not have other responsibilities. The way I got through was sheer blood, sweat, and tears. I would stay up all night. I drank copious cups of coffee. I limited going out and felt guilty taking any breaks. I worked, worked, and worked some more.

That summer between the first and second year, I fell apart. I was actually totally burned out but didn't realize it. I remember going back to my parents' house in the country and just sleeping. I was beyond exhausted and felt like I had chronic fatigue syndrome. My grandparents were visiting from Poland at the time, and they were worried there was something wrong with me. I visited doctors, but my blood work was fine. I also considered completely dropping out of the program, but it honestly felt like too much work trying to figure out alternatives of what I could do.

I remember having a cold that would not subside. I had a total lack of energy, a total lack of interest in anything, and was at a loss of what to do. My passion and drive for success was totally gone. I did not recognize myself.

I did go back in second year, and perhaps because I had slept so much of the summer or because I no longer "cared" to be the best, that year was different. Not caring as much also gave me permission to have some fun. In the second year, I went out with my friends in the program, we skipped classes, we took breaks, we laughed, we danced, and well, something magical happened—I was not only happier, but I actually did better academically. Not staying up, not trying too hard, and taking breaks actually helped me to better handle the bombardment of case studies, reports, presentations, tests, and exams.

To be clear, this chapter is not about "caring less" about your work, it is about caring more about yourself.

Many type A, successful individuals don't know how to set boundaries to recover from their heavy demands. They do, do, do, and work, work, work—and then fall apart. Technology that was supposed to create more time for us has instead tied us to work around the clock and made boundary setting even harder.

What you will discover in this lesson is the concept of work recovery: how setting boundaries will enable you to maintain your energy levels, make you more resilient, and help you perform better at whatever you do, just like I did in the second year of my program.

So if you feel exhausted, stressed, or like you can't catch up, this is your sign to make changes. You can be successful without burning yourself out. Please don't wait to get sick to take this content seriously.

Ready?

The goal in this chapter is to show you that setting boundaries and disconnecting are ways to actually increase your performance, improve your resilience, and enhance your happiness.

Let's start by revisiting our concept of resilience. We often have a militaristic view of resilience. Culturally, we tend to believe that if we work harder, longer, and are tougher, we will be more successful.

New research demonstrates just the opposite. A resilient child, or adult for that matter, is one who is well rested. For example, research shows what we intuitively know to be true. If you stay up all night cramming for an important exam, you are less likely to do well. Staying up and being exhausted is self-defeating in terms of memory recall and brain function in general. Moreover, as we learned in the Sleep Deep chapter, you are then a danger to yourself and others on the road, not to mention you'll have a much lower ability to emotionally self-regulate.

So, the problem is not that we aren't determined or gritty enough; the problem comes from a misunderstanding of what it means to be resilient. Recall from the first chapters that **being resilient is having our batteries charged**! Your phone if unplugged for too long does NOT work and neither do you. It is so simple. Resilient individuals have habits and behaviors that make them resilient, and a key habit is resting and restoring.

In my yoga therapy program, my teachers repeatedly shared that when they prescribe "rest" to a client (we call them students), the students in Canada generally put up a fight. In India, this is not their experience. Why is that?

THE TRUTH ABOUT OVERWORKING IN NORTH AMERICA

Let's dive into our North American tendency to work long hours.

It seems to me that Canada and the US are unique in that people want to work longer and harder to get more money, position, power. On the other hand, I have a good friend whose husband is from Germany. I am amazed at how he negotiates his raises. He is very accomplished and good at what he does. When offered a promotion or salary increase, he often trades it for more time off. He is not worried that he will lose his job or his opportunities to get promoted. In fact, he says the stress that goes along with the most senior positions is not worth it, and he would rather stay where he is and enjoy life. Research documents that Europeans tend to value their work–life balance more. It illustrates something more—the direct correlation between the lack of a true break from work and the increased frequency of both health and safety problems.

The European Heart Journal, for example, reported that compared with people who did not work overtime, people who worked ten or more hours a day had a 60 percent higher risk of heart-related issues including death from heart disease, nonfatal heart attacks, and angina. Further, working in jobs with regular overtime is associated with a 61 percent higher risk of accidents compared to jobs without overtime. Working at least twelve hours per day was associated with a 37 percent increased accident rate.

There are thousands of research studies and articles that demonstrate that long working hours are linked with bad health, lower productivity, strained relationships, poor parenting, and divorce.

How did it come to this?

In the last two decades, the internet and ability to work from home or anywhere, anytime has changed our perception and volume of work. Then Covid pushed us over the edge. It used to be that overworking was identified by long hours at the office, missed family dinners, and weekends away from the family. Now, work can all be done from home and a lot of it just on your phone. This totally blurs the line between personal time and work time. Instead of physically being absent, we are now mentally and emotionally absent (remember the term "phubbing") during personal time as we answer one more email or take a "quick important call." It's a balancing act most of us realize is impossible to maintain.

Technology, while great, has blurred the long-established line between work and family and home and rest. Yes, it allows for work flexibility, which I truly appreciate, but in some cases, it has taken over our personal lives.

In fact, in a great article by Shawn Achor (the funny positivity researcher), I learned that not decompressing or taking a break has a financial bottom-line impact on the organizations we work for. He states, as does *Science Daily*, that a lack of work recovery is costing the US workforce over $62 billion in lost productivity. Ouch!

"Resilience is about how you recharge, not how you endure," Achor says.

"Just because work stops," Achor continues, "it doesn't mean we are recovering. We 'stop' work sometimes at 5 p.m., but then we spend the night wrestling with solutions to work problems, talking about our work over dinner, and falling asleep thinking about how much work we'll do tomorrow." This is definitely not recovering from work.

So what is work recovery?

Given the remote work revolution, we really need a new definition for work recovery. Here is one I have pieced together from various sources: Work recovery is a process of detaching completely from work (including thinking about work) and engaging in practices that help restore you physically, mentally, and emotionally to pre-stressor levels. It is a skill as it requires you to know when to step away from work, what practices work best for your recovery, and then to actually do it.

Let's recall our opening quote from author Anne Lamott: "Almost everything will work again if you unplug it for a few minutes, including you."

FIVE STRATEGIES TO HELP YOU RECHARGE

Let's dive into some strategies for recharging our batteries.

As we have discovered, one of the challenges we face is that our culture doesn't seem to place a high amount of value on idle time. We feel we should fill every moment. In the face of this, it can be hard to rest, relax, and recharge. As a result, most of us go home at the end of the day without a plan for how to let go of the day's events and shift over to another mindset.

Here are five strategies or best practices you can play with to break this cycle and recharge in your down time.

STRATEGY 1: Manage your energy, not only your time

Time is finite. We all have twenty-four hours a day with which to sleep, eat, work, play, and connect with the people who are meaningful to us. We can become stressed when we start to allocate time in a day for all the things that are important. Another way to consider thinking about all we have to do is to manage our energy in addition to our time.

A power plant generates energy—so do you.

Your body is much like a power plant in that you generate your energy—you don't just have energy. Adopting strategies that maximize your energy are key. Of equal importance is also creating rituals to help you refresh your energy levels when they get low. Instead of reaching for a cookie and coffee at 3 p.m., as I did for years, notice your energy is low and take a break. Go for a five-minute walk, run up and down the stairs a few times, or put on a five-minute meditation at your desk. I tell my clients to stand up, and as they breathe in, to rise on their tippy-toes and lift their arms over their head and then hold for five. It is a very energizing dynamic asana to repeat six times.

The good news here is that we have already explored and hopefully implemented some best practices that augment your energy in Resilience Keystone I.

Physical mastery and improved energy

As a refresher, in Keystone I, we reviewed the benefits of eating consciously, sleeping deep, moving often, and breathing slowly as strategies for building our physical mastery and thereby augmenting our resilience. All of these practices will boost your energy levels. You can't create more than twenty-four hours in a day, but you can create how much energy you have.

The purpose of creating more energy and focus is to get your work done at work and leave it there. The worst-case scenario is where you have no energy and drag out the work during the day and then have to drag it home. Become a super-charged bunny—eating well, sleeping well, and moving often will energize you to get done what you need to at work and allow you to leave the rest so that you can recharge at home.

Take regular breaks for energy renewal

It is equally important to take regular breaks in the day for your renewal.

Intermittent breaks from work, regardless how micro they are, result in enhanced productivity and work performance. The length of break is less important than the quality. The key is to completely disconnect from work. Draw on things we learned in other chapters to recharge. Consider going for a quick walk outside to get some fresh air and vitamin D. Listen to a stand-up comedian on your phone and have a good belly laugh. Connect with a colleague or call a family member. Don't talk about work. Do a random act of kindness. Stretch, do some diaphragmatic breathing, or meditate.

The value of such breaks is grounded in our physiology. Ultradian rhythms refer to 90- to 120-minute cycles during which our bodies slowly move from a high-energy state to a lower one. The exact time can vary from person to person but follows the same mechanism. Toward the end of each cycle, the body craves a period of rest. Typical signals include restlessness, hunger, yawning, and difficulty concentrating, but many of us ignore them and keep on going, which is what can lead to burnout.

The better strategy is to look out for this and use it as a reason to break. You will actually get more done in the long run.

STRATEGY 2: Minimize distractions . . . all distractions

Distractions at work drain our energy and reduce productivity. Similarly, and very importantly, distractions during recovery impair our ability to refresh ourselves and replenish our energy reserves.

Distractions hurt you more than you realize.

As we discussed in earlier lessons, multitasking is a myth. Multitasking diminishes productivity and drains our mental energy. We can only focus on one thing at a time.

According to a *Harvard Business Review* article entitled "Manage Your Energy, Not Your Time," "a temporary shift in attention from one task to another increases the amount of time necessary to finish the task by 25 percent, a phenomenon known as switching time."

I noticed this myself, especially when working on big projects. I have a tendency to become distracted by email and social media notifications, text messages, and anything that beeps at me. It can get ridiculous. What is more ridiculous is that it's hard to get back to what I was focused on. Sometimes I forget where I was. Now I have a strategy: When I need to get work done, I shut off all my notifications, including my phone. I set a timer for myself, usually for between forty and sixty minutes. I tell myself (like I would a child) that after the set time period, I can have a break.

It has made all the difference. I am much more productive now and feel less frustrated by my own behavior. So consider shutting off notifications and allocating work time and email time.

STRATEGY 3: Set firm boundaries and transition mindfully

Your boundaries are your self-imposed limits or the rules you set for yourself to ensure that you get the recovery period you need.

Your transition is the period of time required to switch from work to rest. By making this a defined ritual, your body and mind can more quickly begin to recover.

Set your limits

Work stays at work.

Put your phone away or limit your access to it; let your phone recharge its battery.

Create a transition ritual from work to home as we discussed in the mindfulness section.

Setting limits is hard and completely at odds with many corporate cultures. Many firms say that they want you to have balance, but at the same time, management may be setting a bad example by sending emails at night or on weekends. The simple fact is that if you plan to wait for your organization to set limits for you, then you are going to be waiting a very, very long time. You need to set your own limits.

The best place to start is with the concept of (1) work stays at work. It doesn't matter if work is a place or not. Stick to your workday, and when it's over, it's over. (2) Put away your phone or limit access to work material. Your phone needs a recharge and so do you. Sign out of work accounts, turn off notifications, and even leave your laptop at work. If you need to be reachable in case of legitimate work emergencies, develop strategies with colleagues for being in touch. The trick here is that you need to develop these limits and communicate them to others. Finally, (3) create a transition time from work to recovery. For example, don't use your commute to continue work calls or email on the subway. Use the time to decompress and disconnect, think about what you want to do to recharge, and how want to show up at home.

STRATEGY 4: Prioritize and plan ahead

Strategy number four builds on boundary setting by prioritizing and planning ahead. The reality is that none of us can have a balanced life if we measure it on a daily basis. Our suggestion is to manage it on a weekly basis. A week is long enough to absorb big workdays where the focus is almost exclusively on work; however, it's a short enough timeframe to ensure that you get balance.

Back to first things first.

One of the tools we encourage you to use is the concept presented by Stephen Covey in his book *First Things First*.

Covey describes setting priorities as the most important aspect of successful (personal) improvement. No matter how efficiently you do your work, if you're doing the wrong thing, nothing will really improve.

Determine your priorities, what work will create the most impact or value over the long run, then do that. Then, most importantly, say NO to other things. The key to boundary setting is to know your priorities and say no to the rest. Remember when we spoke about a "not-to-do" list in the foundations module? Go back and review that overwhelm audit chapter again.

Also, consider having a planning session at the end of every week. Take half an hour on Sunday evening to look at your week. Look at what deadlines are ahead and schedule tasks with appropriate work hours to complete the tasks (do not include home time to complete the tasks). Plan your recovery activities for the week and share those with your partner or family.

Again, focus on tasks with the most long-term impact.

STRATEGY 5: Give yourself some "me time"

Ah, what a luxury, especially if you work full time, have kids, a spouse, and aging parents to look after. Me time is a much dreamed about notion because people bemoan that they don't have any. I know I did! Interestingly, studies show that me time doesn't have to be grand or even solitary. The key is that you engage in freely chosen non-work activities.

Me time

A study on "me time" by Dr. Almuth McDowall at Birkbeck University, for example, showed that me time enhances overall well-being and makes you a more engaged and productive employee.

Dr. McDowall's research suggests "If people take time out to recharge their batteries and experience the time as high quality, it reaps benefits for their own psychological well-being, their family relationships, and for their employers as they are more likely to perform better at work."

In fact, the study's results demonstrated that the people who created some quality me time were more engaged at work, as well as being happier about their life overall.

Self-care is not self-indulgent, it is a disease-prevention strategy that makes you more productive, resilient, and likely more fun.

So that brings us to the end of the strategies to recharge.

As we conclude this lesson, I want to highlight an important fact—recharging or energy renewal is not limited to weekends and vacations. It really is something you can do daily, even hourly in the office while at work. In fact, it is all about self-awareness. Notice when you are stressed, have low energy, or anxiety. If you do, then that is precisely the moment to give yourself a break. Use your mindfulness tools to both notice your state and then change it through breathing, meditating, or going for a walk.

Remember, self-care is disease prevention. If you don't take care of you by setting priorities, boundaries, and saying no, no one else will, and you won't be very resilient or successful in the long run.

Now it's time to Do the Work and BE Resilient

This week's challenge exercise is to set some boundaries and chill out. Isn't that nice homework to have?

Seriously, I really, really encourage you to make the decision to recharge and set some work limitations, especially with email, as it has a nasty way of keeping us connected to work.

THE REST AND RECHARGE CHALLENGE

Please take a moment to review the key practices presented to rest and recharge. This is an area of weakness for me, so I am choosing to really focus on this lesson and give myself more me time. Please choose ONE thing and commit to it. This is fun and pleasant. Enjoy!

1. Manage your energy, not only your time.

2. Minimize distractions.

3. Set firm boundaries and transition from task to task mindfully.

4. Prioritize and plan ahead.

5. Give yourself some "me time"—remember to plan for it!

The last word on resting and recharging:

Self-care is not self-indulgent, it is a disease-prevention strategy that makes you more productive, resilient, and likely more fun.

RESILIENCE KEYSTONE III: INTENTIONAL ORIENTATION

*"It is only those that live intentionally that can accomplish
and come to the significance meant for them."*
—SUNDAY ADELAJA

Welcome to the final stretch. I hope you are feeling stronger physically, mentally, and emotionally after having adopted so many new habits.

As always, when we begin a new section, I have you recall that the American Psychological Association states that "Resilience is NOT a trait that people either have or do not have. It involves behaviors, thoughts, and actions that can be learned and developed in anyone."

Also, recall that Keystone I focused on developing our physical well-being. We can't think fast and be resilient when we are physically unwell. We then moved onto developing our self-awareness through practices that make us more mindful of our behaviors, thoughts, feelings, and actions.

In this section, we learn that resilient individuals also tend to have an intentional orientation. What that means is they have habits, behaviors, and take actions that are supportive and congruent with their intentions.

WHAT DOES INTENTIONAL ORIENTATION MEAN?

For the purposes of this book, when I speak of someone having an intentional orientation, I mean they engage in the mindful process of designing their life in a purposeful way, one that is congruent with their vision, values, and beliefs. But it goes deeper than just setting congruent goals to be accomplished. Part of intention is connecting and aligning with an invisible power or force field that is greater than us to guide us along the way.

In Keystone III we will develop intentionality.

We start with a chapter on intentional living and what it looks like in practice. We will then dive into another aspect of the power of intention, and that is spirituality.

Wayne Dyer, in the book *The Power of Intention*, writes, "At our Source, we are formless energy, and in that formless vibrating spiritual field of energy, intention resides."

I want to point out that this chapter is distinct from the others. Specifically, Chapter 13 on intentional living is integrated with the challenge exercise. What that means is that you will fill out the challenge exercise sheet while you read.

Take this time to think through your best life and best self. We don't often create the space to do so.

As you go through the intentional living lessons, a reminder to continue to keep your WHY for doing this work in focus. See how your WHY weaves into your plan for an intentional life.

Maintain your morning routine. Recall all top performers have a morning routine during which they determine what they want to achieve in the day and how they want to show up in the world. The morning routine IS an intentional living practice. It is also the best time to commune with Source.

I am so excited for you to dive into this keystone.

Chapter 13
LIVE WITH INTENTION

"Intent is not a thought or an object or a wish.
Intent is what can make a man succeed when his thoughts tell him
that he is defeated. It operates in spite of the warrior's indulgence.
Intent is what makes him invulnerable. Intent is what sends a sha-
man through a wall, through space, to infinity."
—Carlos Castañeda

I was always a "good girl." I got good marks, had nice friends, and followed the path that was laid before me. I progressed from elementary to high school successfully. In high school, I excelled. My marks were great, my teachers liked me, and most suggested I become a lawyer, as I was also fairly outspoken in class. I went to university with that path in mind, never really contemplating whether I was all that interested in law. I did not notice that none of the books I gravitated toward or the activities outside of academia I got involved in had anything remotely to do with law or even justice.

Although I did not go on to law school after my undergrad, I went on to do a Master in Business. Again, I turned away from my side hobbies and interests and focused my time on what seemed the external world perceived as successful. An MBA sounded important to me, so it was worthy of pursuit. I focused on finance, accounting, marketing, strategy, and how to become a manager or leader in a large organization. The fact that I spent any time I had in the holistic health, wellness, and spirituality section at the local bookstore did not get through to me.

I graduated and immediately got a job as a senior program manager in a very large organization, the federal government. Here was another ladder to follow, and it seemed like a solid and good one. My parents approved, as did society.

It was probably after about the first two weeks something happened—I woke up. I was twenty-five and looked around the sea of cubicles and my work and thought: I hate this! I was bored and found it hard to get motivated and perform, as this was not my passion at all. When after three years my director spoke to me about a management trainee program that would commit me to a lifelong career working for the feds, I decided to RUN. I saw this was not my dream. I didn't even know what my dream was, but it was not this, not for me.

Much to my parents' chagrin, I fully quit my secure job without having anything else lined up. The first thing I did after my last day of work was take a Tony Robbins course on finding my purpose. It was not online, this was the early 2000s, so I had to wait for the binder with tape recordings and a workbook to arrive by snail mail. But when I finally received it, I sat down in my little one-bedroom apartment and for the first time in my life, on my own—without the influence of society, parents, teachers, or anyone—I dreamed about who I wanted to be when "I grew up."

I still have that workbook somewhere. It was strange, as what came out of the elaborate exercise was that I wanted to teach and help others to find and reach their dreams and potential. I came up with a title for myself, wrote it out boldly, and taped it on my fridge: "Human Potential Development Consultant."

Life coaching barely existed then, but I did take a course through CoachU. They were located in California, so I called in to a weekly lesson. But I still had no idea how to make money in this new chosen career. Having said that, the title posted on my fridge became a guiding post and my life, and a career began to unravel. And it did so more authentically, not necessarily more easily, but more with a different energy—one of possibilities and excitement.

Having this new vision and tuning into me as opposed to a default path turned my life around. It also made me more resilient to the bumps along the way to realizing my vision.

Today, we are going to dive into living with intention. Resilient individuals tend to be intentionally oriented. What that means is that they set intentions and deliberately take action in line with those intentions. This chapter is going to challenge you in different ways as you will soon discover. It will leverage your self-awareness and deliberate action practices in order to have you consider a new paradigm for how to be your best self.

What you will discover in this lesson is:

- Why intentional living is critical and how it relates to resilience.
- What intentional living entails.
- The five steps to creating an intentional life.
- How to set yourself up for success.

Imagine creating your ideal life and being your best self. Imagine living in congruence with your values and taking deliberate action in alignment with your vision and goals. In this chapter, we will do just that. Please note, this lesson will be different from the others in that I will guide you through the exercises right in the body of the lesson, like good ole Tony did with me way back when. I will prep you for each activity and then ask you to pause and complete the exercise before moving on to the next.

Ready? Take a deep breath and let's begin.

What is the goal of this chapter?

It is to use the tools provided to start living intentionally. Specifically, it is to create a life and lifestyle that is congruent with your values and ideals.

WHY LIVE INTENTIONALLY?

Many of us are living by default. We spend our lives driven by habits that are not serving our real goals. In fact, I would argue many, if not most, living beings spend their entire life driven by instincts and habits, in a state of autopilot. Like I did. It is like our lives are a collection of reactions to the people and circumstances within which we operate.

When we live by default, we are not living in a way that is consistent with our values, beliefs, and desires. I think of a ping-pong ball being bounced around by external forces as opposed to our internal vision.

Even worse, we think this is just the way it is and that we are powerless to change the course of our life.

Research shows that resilient individuals and top performers, in general, tend to take ownership over their lives by having an intentional orientation. Note the Resilient by Design model. Having an intentional orientation—knowing where you are going and why—is fundamental to being resilient. Resilient individuals also develop habits and behaviors that are in support of their intentions.

Joshua Becker, a well-known minimalist who inspires millions around the world to find greater fulfillment in life by owning fewer possessions, commands: "Don't just drift through life. Live intentionally and on purpose."

WHAT IS LIVING INTENTIONALLY?

Let's get more specific: Intentional living is a mindful (there is that word again) process of designing your life in a purposeful way; one that is congruent with your values, beliefs, and desires. It requires you to be self-aware, to know your fundamental values, beliefs, and desires, and to be willing to align your behaviors, actions, and choices with them.

When put into practice every day, intentional living has the power to change your life. Intentional living is a lifestyle based on your conscious choice to live according to your values or beliefs as opposed to on autopilot. It is achieved by knowing yourself and becoming an active participant in the flow of life.

It is also about making choices in our lives with intent. It is a thoughtful consideration of the pros and cons of each choice and the impact our choices make on ourselves, our families, and our world. It entails carefully choosing your thoughts, words, and actions.

To evaluate choices, it is important to have a clear understanding of our value system. And to have what I like to call a life strategy.

I worked for several large and small organizations after my federal government stint. I even facilitated strategy sessions. Every organization, big or small, has a corporate strategy. They have a vision of who they are and where they are going and then figure out how to get there. Some companies do this badly, others well. But they would not survive without them. Just like all these organizations, I realized that we, too, need to know where we are going, how we are going to get there, and what the end result will look like. It turns out resilient people know this for themselves.

So let's compare organizational strategies and life strategies that intentionally oriented individuals have.

1.   Organizations have a mission statement—a one sentence statement describing the reason an organization exists. Similarly, intentionally oriented individuals articulate what is important to them. They may even have a personal mission statement that provides clarity around their purpose and defines who they are and how they live.

2.   Organizations identify their values. Being firmly aware of our values serves as a powerful decision-making tool for us.

3. Organizations articulate their three- to five-year vision—they define where they are heading. This is a critical success factor for us as well. How do you know you reached your destination when you haven't truly defined it?

4. Companies then create a strategy. An organizational strategy articulates the how—how a company will reach their vision and "win in their playing field," as Roger Martin, the former dean of the Rotman School of Management and strategist says. We also must determine our strategy for how we are going to reach our vision and live our values. Setting goals is a great tool to get us there.

5. Finally, a strategy needs an operational plan and action. And we need to do the work and take action to make our vision a reality. Recall we have to "do the work to become resilient."

So let's go create a life strategy via the five steps to living intentionally.

I invite you to take some time with me as your guide on the side to clarify your purpose, values, vision, and goals and become an intentional creator in your life. If you have made it this far in the book, this process is the glue that will hold everything together. And it will also help you carry your new best practices forward.

As I mentioned earlier, this lesson is distinct from the ones prior in that I will present the step and then ask you to pause and do the exercise. The idea is that by the end of the chapter you will have clarity around your ideal life and how to create it. I find the potential buried in this exercise very exciting. Let's do this!

STEP 1 TO LIVING INTENTIONALLY:
Know what is important to you

At first we called this step knowing your purpose, then knowing your WHY, then landed on knowing what is important to you. Here's the idea: We exist on this earth for some undetermined period of time. During that time, we do things. Some of these things are important. Some of them are unimportant. And those important things give our lives meaning and happiness. The unimportant ones basically just kill time and maybe us a little bit too. Intentional living works by creating boundary lines around your life with what is important to you or your why or purpose, if you want to use that language.

I believe that we often let the world define what is important to us before we even know we have the choice. There is a moment in our lives when we learn that what we wear, drive, or love, or who we are isn't enough or the right kind of beauty or talent, and our focus is unintentionally defined to live up to external standards. So we break our backs and our hearts to meet an expectation that is impossible to meet and that was never meant to be the context of our lives.

Let's not do that here. Let's start fresh by asking: ***What do I want to do with my time that is important to me?***

This is an infinitely better question to ask than what is your purpose. It's far more manageable and it doesn't have all the baggage that the "life purpose" question does. There's no reason or benefit for you to be contemplating the cosmic significance of your life while sitting on your couch eating chips all day. Rather, you should be getting off your couch and discovering what feels important to you.

Why? Because those whose actions are intent-based always seem to have more stamina, more grit, and more optimism. We have all heard the expression "passion fuels power." Those with a passion or who are taking a stand for something are always more powerful than those who do not. Our lives become meaningful through the impact we make on others, more so than living and working just for ourselves. A passion is often in service of others.

So what is your passion? What is important to you?

I do not want you to get stuck here and then not complete the lesson. Trying to follow your passion or follow your bliss, as Joseph Campbell says, can trip people up. I know I used to panic when I asked myself "What is my bliss? What is my bliss?" I had no idea! Sitting on a patio drinking cocktails with friends didn't seem like a deep and meaningful answer.

So instead of asking you to ruminate on those heavy questions, I use some lighthearted questions that shed light on what is important to you and serve as a guide to your purpose.

In her book *Big Magic*, Elizabeth Gilbert points out that every endeavor involves sacrifice.

Question 1. What are you willing to struggle for? Or in Gilbert's words, "Eat a shit sandwich for?"

Everything includes some sort of cost. Nothing is pleasurable or uplifting all the time. So, the question becomes: What struggle or sacrifice are you willing to tolerate?

Ultimately, what determines our ability to stick with something we care about is our ability to handle the rough patches and ride out the inevitable rotten days. What unpleasant experiences are you able to handle? Are you able to stay up all night painting or coding? Are you able to have people laugh you off the stage over and over again until you get it right? Are you able to sacrifice your time to write a book or a play?

What are you willing to struggle for? Take a moment and answer this question here:

....

....

....

Question 2. If forced to stand in front of a crowd with a megaphone and shout about something, what would be your thing?

This question really hits home for me. It makes me realize that there are a couple of issues that really, really get me going. For example, I get so upset by all the crappy, addictive food that is marketed and readily available for our kids! Even now as I write this, my blood starts to boil. I must stop myself from going off on a tangent about it. What are those issues for you?

If forced to stand in front of a crowd with a megaphone and shout about something, what would be your thing? Take a moment and answer this question here:

....

....

....

Here's another one that really helps clarify my passions:

Question 3. When you walk into a bookstore, what section do you always gravitate toward? What podcasts do you listen to? What newsletters are you signed up for? What newsletters do you actually open?

Although I studied business, during my MBA, my friends knew to always find me in the natural health and nutrition section at a bookstore. In fact, they joked it was my office. Too bad I didn't see then what is so clear now!

When you walk into a bookstore, what section do you always gravitate toward? Take a moment and answer this question here:

Question 4. If you knew you had one year to live and had to do something aside from roll yourself up in a ball, what would you do? Who would you spend time with? What would you actually do? Where would you go? How would you spend your precious time? This is a question we have heard over and over again, yet we rarely take the time to thoughtfully answer it.

If you knew you had one year to live and had to do something aside from roll yourself up in a ball, what would you do? Take a moment and answer this question here:

Based on your answers to those four questions, what is emerging as important to you?

STEP 2 TO LIVING INTENTIONALLY:
Identify your core values

Intentional individuals are values-driven.

Values, to be clear, are a little different from your passion or issues of importance to you. When we speak about values, we are talking about deeply held principles, ideals, or beliefs that people hold or adhere to when making decisions. Whereas organizations express their values through their cultural behaviors, individuals express their values through personal behaviors.

Values stand at the very core of human decision-making. They are a powerful tool. I did a rigorous values-based exercise about five years ago. My values emerged crystal clear. What also emerged was the fact that I was living out of congruence with several key values. I made a decision, a big one, to change my life and start living in accordance with my values. Whenever I waver now, I come back to them. As the values still resonate deeply, I hold them close.

Finally, I want to clarify that values can be positive or potentially limiting. For example, the positive value of "trust" is fundamental for creating a cohesive group culture. On the other hand, the potentially limiting value of "being liked" can cause people to compromise their integrity in order to satisfy their need for approval.

Peak-performing individuals and companies are values-driven; conversely, it is virtually impossible to maintain peak performance when one's most basic values are not nourished, or worse, "undervalued."

You can only be truly authentic when living according to the principles that matter most to you. This applies to your personal life and your work life and is especially true when considering how you lead others.

The best way to identify your values is to ask yourself:

- Who am I?
- What do I believe in?
- What do I stand for?

There are no right or wrong answers.

Think about the things that make you feel you are really doing what you were put on this earth to do. Which activities leave you feeling fulfilled and satisfied?

Consider what it is about them that makes them so special. It is usually the fact that a core value is being met—something like challenge, fun, contribution, or order.

Now let's do the work and answer those questions. Again, do it now as opposed to leaving it for later. Later is always later and it doesn't get done. Well, that's the case with me anyway. Many of us have a tendency to push the work away, even the work of creating our life. There is power in action and there is power in now.

Pause and complete the following to arrive at your core values.

- Think about which activities leave you feeling fulfilled and satisfied.
- What is it about them that makes them so special? It is usually the fact that a core value is being met.

Describe what is becoming apparent to you.

....

....

....

....

....

....

....

....

....

....

INVENTORY OF VALUES

Here's another way to identify key values. Use ticks and crosses to mark off values. There may be some additional personal values that are unique to you, so don't be limited by the list. Add anything else that just feels right.

ACCEPTANCE	COOPERATION	ETHICS
ACHIEVEMENT	COLLABORATION	EXCELLENCE
ADVANCEMENT & PROMOTION	CREATIVITY	EXCITEMENT
ADVENTURE	DECISIVENESS	FAIRNESS
AFFECTION	DEMOCRACY	FAME
ALTRUISM	DESIGN	FAMILY
ARTS	DISCOVERY	HAPPINESS
AWARENESS	DIVERSITY	FAST-PACED LIFESTYLE
BEAUTY	ENVIRONMENTAL AWARENESS	FREEDOM
CHALLENGE	ECONOMIC SECURITY	FRIENDSHIP
CHANGE	EDUCATION	FUN
COMMUNITY	EFFECTIVENESS	GRACE
COMPASSION	EFFICIENCY	GROWTH
COMPETENCE	ELEGANCE	HARMONY
COMPETITION	ENTERTAINMENT	HEALTH
COMPLETION	ENLIGHTENMENT	HELPING OTHERS
CONNECTEDNESS	EQUALITY	HELPING SOCIETY

HONESTY

HUMOR

IMAGINATION

IMPROVEMENT

INDEPENDENCE

INFLUENCING

INNER HARMONY

INSPIRATION

INTEGRITY

INTELLECT

KNOWLEDGE

LEADERSHIP

LEARNING

LOYALTY

MAGNIFICENCE

MAKING A DIFFERENCE

MASTERY

MEANINGFUL WORK

MINISTERING

MONEY

NATURE

OPENNESS

PEACE

PERSONAL DEVELOPMENT

PERSONAL EXPRESSION

PLANNING

PLAY

PLEASURE

POWER

PRIVACY

QUALITY RECOGNITION

RELATIONSHIPS

RELIGION

REPUTATION

RESPONSIBILITY & ACCOUNTABILITY

RISK SAFETY & SECURITY

SELF-RESPECT

SENSIBILITY

SERENITY

SERVICE

SOPHISTICATION

SPARK

SPIRITUALITY

STABILITY

STATUS

SUCCESS

TEACHING

TENDERNESS

VARIETY

WEALTH

Other values that are not on this list:

....

....

....

Out of all the values you highlighted, choose the **five** most important to you.

....

....

....

Consider to what extent these values are expressed in your life or work today.

....

....

....

....

STEP 3 TO LIVING INTENTIONALLY: Create a vision

A vision is a picture or idea you have in your mind of yourself, your family, your business, your organization, or anything that is going to happen. A clear vision helps you pursue dreams and achieve goals—it is an idea of the future. A vision that is clear will open your mind to the endless possibilities of the future. It will also help you to overcome obstacles in the way and help you to hold on when times are tough. When we read inspirational stories about people who rose above the toughest circumstances, they always had and relied on a vision. Think Gandhi, Martin Luther King Jr., Viktor Frankl. Most understand why successful companies have a vision. It is a target upon which a leader focuses resources and energy.

A vision is of equal importance to a person. A vision that is well defined helps you to focus and create the life of your intentions. It connects your actions with your passions, values, and greatest potentials. And finally, it helps guide decision-making and problem solving, always keeping you moving in the right direction.

Your vision should embody your values and your view of the future without being too generic. Some people like to create vision boards. When I look back on some of mine, it's almost eerie how much of the pictures materialized.

The point of having a vision is so you know why you're doing what you do, and you are happier doing it. Again, this comes back to creating a future based on your values. Our ability to envision in the mind's eye what we hope to create gives us a real leg up in actually creating it.

A question I'm commonly asked is whether your vision can change. Yes, of course. Your vision will evolve, just like you will, over time.

Having a vision forces you to answer:

- Who you are and who you want to be.
- What you want to get out of life.
- What you want to be remembered for.

When creating a vision, keep in mind what you want.

Sometimes we don't know what we want, so imagine what feels good. What are you attracted to? Notice what you notice and how that makes you feel. This is a mindfulness, self-awareness exercise. Also, remember that anything is possible with a vision, so think BIG. Dream. Imagine. Brainstorm. Play with what feels exciting and good. Focus on your values and the things that give your life purpose and meaning. Finally, and most importantly, **do not put limits on your dreams.**

Let's use a guided meditation to get warmed up for the visioning exercise you are about to do. This meditation will take no longer than five minutes. Ideally, find a space now where you will be alone and undisturbed for the next five minutes and then for ten to fifteen minutes as you write out your ideal vision.

Guided meditation:

Close your eyes. Find a comfortable position and allow yourself to relax and simply be. Take a deep breath in, and as you breathe out, let go of everything but your breath. Take another deep breath and connect to your purest, highest inner self.

This guided meditation will help you to envision your ideal self and perfect future. We will tap into those feelings and emotions of the future we wish to create. As you allow your body to become still, bring your attention back to the fact that you are breathing. Become aware of the movement of your breath as it comes into your body and as it leaves your body. Relax. Breathe in gently. Exhale fully.

As you sit here and continue to breathe mindfully, allow the field of your awareness to expand.

Lean out three years. Through your mind's eye, start to formulate a picture of your perfect future. Feel the happy emotions as you visualize what it is you wish to have. What does it look like three years from today? Think about your ideal life.

Think BIG!

Dream BIG!

Do not include feasibility, reality, or how. Simply picture what you want.

See it. Feel it. Notice who is there with you.

Resist focusing on how you will achieve any of it.

Define the fulfillment of your dream with all your senses:

What do you see?

What do you hear?

What are others saying about you?

What sensations are you experiencing?

Let all possibilities in. Energize your vision with emotion. Feel how it feels to have what you want.

Take a deep breath in and feel the future take root. As you exhale, clear away the uncertainty or doubt.

Inhale, root—exhale, clear.

Inhale, root the ideal—exhale, clear any resistance.

Once more time: inhale, root the perfect future—exhale, let go of anything that does not serve the vision.

Take another deep breath in—release. Open your eyes.

Like as suggested in the mindfulness chapter, consider recording yourself reading this script and then listen and experience it as a mediation.

We are now ready to do the **Painted Picture** exercise.

I don't recall exactly where I first encountered this exercise, but I have been doing it with clients and in workshops for years. It is so much fun! Without judgment, write out a big, beautiful, ideal version of your life and of yourself on a set date three years from now. Write it as if you have already achieved it.

- How does it look?
- How does it feel?
- What do others say about you?

Now let me guide you through creating it. Again, do it now as opposed to leaving it for later.

Create your vision: The Painted Picture

Lean out three years into the future and think about your ideal life. Play with possibilities—dream, imagine, and try on wild ideas. Then, without judgment, write out a big, beautiful, ideal version of your life and of yourself.

Remember it is critical here that you **do not** get caught up in the *how* aspect. Your focus is on the *what*. Describe:

- Your career:
  - What are you doing; with whom and how?
  - How much do you work and how much do you earn?
  - Who are you serving?

- Your family, your homelife
- Your friends
- Your leisure, hobbies, self-care
- Your health and well-being
- How you feel and how you make others feel
- Your community
- Your weekends
- Do you wake up early or late?
- Highly scheduled or not?
- Pets? Etc.?

You have some space here but I suggest doing this exercise on several large pieces of paper or in a journal. You may even paint your picture or create it into a vision board.

Welcome back! As you sit with your vision, this quote from one of my favorite authors and teachers, Wayne Dyer, is particularly relevant: "It is my belief that you are never given the power to dream without the equivalent power to manifest that dream and make it your physical reality." Hear! Hear!

STEP 4 TO LIVING INTENTIONALLY:
Set goals congruent with your vision

When you think about what you deeply desire in your life, what do you have to do in order to get from here to there? Or to use Dyer's words, what do you have to do to manifest that dream?

Generally, there is a gap between your vision and where you are now. Goals bridge that gap. They help set the path, much like a GPS helps you get to your chosen destination.

A goal is a broad primary outcome. It is something you want to achieve. You can think of goal setting as figuring out the intermediate outcomes to attain your vision. An action plan is your specific way of achieving that goal. We'll do that in the next exercise. In this exercise, our focus is on identifying our goals.

The process of goal setting

The clearer you are, the easier it will be to focus on making things happen. When you know what you want and why you want it, the doing becomes easier and easier.

Now think about the VISION you created and what you deeply desire in your life. What changes need to take place to get you there?

Ask yourself:

- Who do I have to BE to arrive at my vision?
- What actions can I take to move toward my goal?
- What gaps exist in my knowledge? What do I need to know or learn?
- What spiritual, emotional, personal, financial, social, or physical issues need to be addressed?

Whereas your vision is a big picture, your goals can be specific, measurable, and time bound.

The clearer you are with each of these dimensions, the easier it will be to bring your vision into sharp focus and make it happen.

Cluster your goals

It is also easier to begin if you cluster your goals under these general headings. Most of us will have:

- Health and fitness goals
- Personal development goals
- Career/business/financial goals
- Knowledge / professional development goals
- Contribution/spiritual goals
- Social/family goals
- Travel/adventure/toys goals
- Other

But you do not have to write your goals under each bucket. Do use your Painted Picture in this process, however. Also, identify your top priority goals. They should be measurable and time bound.

Now let's do the work and set goals congruent with our vision. Don't put this off until later. Later is always later, and now is the time to start crafting your future.

Writing down your goals is key to success. By writing down your goals, you become a creator. Failure to write down your goals often means you will forget them or won't focus on them. Have them written down where you can see them every day.

Pause and set goals congruent with your vision exercise.

The clearer you are, the easier it will be to focus on making it happen. When you know what you want and why you want it, the doing becomes easier and easier.

It is also easier to begin if you cluster your goals under the aforementioned general headings. Think back to your Painted Picture. Identify your top priority goals. Please note you do not have to write goals under each bucket.

Health and fitness goals

....

....

....

Personal development goals

....

....

....

Career/business/financial goals

....

....

....

Knowledge / professional development goals

....

....

....

Contribution/spiritual goals

....

....

....

Social/family goals

....

....

....

Travel/adventure/toys goals

....

....

....

Other ....

STEP 5 TO LIVING INTENTIONALLY:
Deliberate action planning

Now that you have determined WHAT you want to achieve and WHY it is important to you, you can plan your course of action. Action planning is figuring out the HOW to achieve the goals and manifest your vision. Some people get stuck on the word manifest, and I considered leaving it out. The reason I didn't is because it highlights an important concept. We create our reality through our thoughts and actions. You have created a vision, and now we are going to outline how you will MANIFEST IT!

3–2–1–Action

Resilient individuals are action oriented. Also, research repeatedly shows that peak performers are masters at execution; they know what their key priorities are and get them done.

Recall the idea from our recharge lesson: time is finite, so we have to use it well.

You may not know all the steps ahead of time, but you will know the next steps that take you in direction you are heading.

Having a vision and goals without a plan of action is like trying to complete a complex project without a project plan.

Personalized action plan

If you've never engaged in action planning, here's how to start. Simply take a goal and break it down into the work or effort required. Here is a list of questions to help you with goal planning:

- What is the specific work or effort required to achieve your goal?
- What time investment is actually required?
- What should your weekly schedule look like to support achieving this goal?
- What obstacles will you face, and how will you respond?

As you can imagine, this process is incredibly revealing as to what it really takes to achieve your goal. Think of action plans as a story of what you'll do to get you to your goal. Choose at least three goals from your list and create your action plan for realizing them.

Now before we jump into action planning, I want us to acknowledge all the reasons why we cannot do or have the things we envision. As we discussed in the chapter on neuroscience, human beings fear change, and our natural inclination is going to be to put up some barriers, even if you do want the change. If you find yourself saying, "Yes, but—" tune in.

I did one of those Landmark Forum boot camp weekends. I loved what they taught about the three-letter word "but." *But* is a powerful little word that can create a dependency where none actually exists. For example:

"I want X . . . but I can't have it because of Y." For example:

"I want more time with my family . . . but my job requires I stay late."

"I want to build a side business . . . but I am too busy."

The *but*, they taught, limits what is possible and creates artificial barriers.

Think of a "but" when it comes to your vision now. Then stop the negative spiral of thoughts and play with shifting "but" to "and."

Replacing "but" with "and" acknowledges that these are two separate facts and opens up possibilities for ACTION.

Let's look at the previous examples.

"I want more time with my family . . . and my job requires I stay late."

"I want to build a side business . . . and I am too busy."

Making this shift causes the brain to acknowledge the points to be separate facts and allows for the possibility that both can be achieved. Can you feel that? Take your *but* statement and play with it now. Do you sense the possibilities created?

This is really about "becoming unreasonable," as Landmark instructors teach. Sounds funny, doesn't it? It is ingrained in us that we must be reasonable, so we create all the reasons why a better way to live and our dreams are not possible. What if we eliminated those excuses? Would that open up possibilities?

The other thing I want to reinforce here is the importance of STARTING NOW and starting before you are ready. Being reasonable is accepting the limitations others and even we ourselves have put in our way. Become unreasonable and start making the changes and taking the actions that move you toward your vision.

Let's do the work. Please take some time to complete the exercise now. Remember to shift your "buts" to "ands" and identify three tangible action steps to take to move your goals forward.

Action planning exercise

Now that you have determined **what** you want to achieve and **why** it is important to you, you can plan your course of action. Action planning is figuring out the **how** to achieve the goal.

If you've never engaged in action planning, here's how to start. Simply take a goal and break it down into the work or effort required. Here is a list of questions to help you with goal planning:

1. What is the specific work or effort required to achieve your goal?

Example: My goal is to get fit and lose 10 lb. I will cut processed sugar out of my life and walk six days a week.

2. What time investment is actually required? What should your weekly schedule look like to support achieving this goal?

Example: To get fit, I will need to take a fast-paced walk thirty minutes a day, six days a week. I will take a more leisurely walk on Sundays.

3. What obstacles will you face and how will you respond?

Example: I love sweets. I will throw out cookies, candies, and sugar from my pantry and not buy any more. I will ask for my husband's support. I will also speak to my colleagues who offer me goodies daily.

As you can imagine, this process is incredibly revealing as to what it really takes to achieve your goal. Think of action plans as a story of what you'll do to get you to your goal. Choose at least three goals from your list and create your action plan for realizing them.

YOUR PERSONALIZED INTENTIONAL ACTION PLAN

Goal (specific, measurable, and time bound)	1	2	3
1. What is the specific work or effort required to achieve my goal?			
2. What time investment is required? What should my weekly schedule look like to support achieving this goal?			
3. What obstacles will I face and how will I respond?			
4. What is the completion date / what date will my goal be realized?			

As we finish this chapter, let's again ponder more wise words from Wayne Dyer: "The secret to manifesting anything that you desire is your willingness and ability to realign yourself so that your inner world is in harmony with the power of intention."

Not only do we have to know and contemplate what we want to create, we have to realign our inner world to be in harmony with it. What that means to me is we have to love ourselves enough to follow the whispering of our hearts. It also means transcending the doubt that will inevitably arise. If you doubt the ability to create the life you want, then that is what you will create more of. Suzanne Eder said, **"What you want, wants you."** Isn't that great?

John C. Maxwell said, "An intentional life embraces only those things that will add to the mission of significance."

What is significant to you? Think about your day and what it is filled with. Imagine that every day you replaced something that doesn't add to your mission of significance with something that does. Just one thing or action each day. Where would your life be six months from now? In three years from now? As we love to say in our programs, do the work and make it real.

The last word on intentional living is:

**To create a life you love, overcome challenges
and be your best, most resilient self, you need to be
intentional. You need a strong sense of purpose or passion,
an awareness of your values, to have a vision,
congruent goals, and to take deliberate action.**

---

*"What man actually needs is not a tensionless state, but rather the
striving and struggling for some goal worthy of him. What he needs
is not the discharge of tension at any cost, but the call of a potential
meaning waiting to be fulfilled by him."*
–Viktor Frankl

Chapter 14
STRENGTHEN YOUR SPIRIT

"Intent is a force that exists in the universe. When sorcerers (those who live of the Source) beckon intent, it comes to them and sets up the path for attainment, which means that sorcerers always accomplish what they set out to do."

–CARLOS CASTAÑEDA

I would be disingenuous if I ended a book on resilience without talking about the "Force," as Castañeda calls it, that I turn to for help, strength, guidance, wisdom, and peace. Whatever you want to call it—Source, God, Universal Love, or the Great Manitou—it really is the foundation of my personal resilience.

I have always been a believer, although I did not believe in organized religion per se. I realized early on that many religions were institutions with man-made rules, often governed by corrupt men. I did not believe that my way to God or Jesus was through a church. I felt the "Force" as a child in nature, by looking in the sky, or listening to my instincts, before I learned to look externally for answers. As an adult, I read voraciously on all things spiritual: I attended mass, prayer circles, meditations, energy healings, entity removal services, and séances. But it was in silence where I discovered that the Force is like an invisibly energy field that we are all connected to, but often not aware of. Like the "Force" in *Star Wars*, it is always there but in a higher vibration than we commonly operate in. In a lower vibration, we often do not see it, feel it, or know that it surrounds us like the air we breathe.

I was at a silent retreat. Probably my third or forth one with my beloved yoga teachers. It was the fall and absolutely stunning outside. Here in Southern Ontario, our autumn is quite beautiful. The leaves had turned color, yet it was still warm out. The retreat center was located on the Bruce Trail, which is the oldest and longest marked hiking trail in Canada. The trail was a forested, winding path. It was hilly, with intermittent streams and logs to cross. We were instructed to walk mindfully as we walked in silence. It was probably day three of the silent retreat, and I had settled into the silence now. It felt like a strange sort of freedom to be with people and not have to talk. I love people, and here in silence I could feel them more than when they spoke to me with words.

I was walking silently along the trail, keeping pace with the group. One foot in front of the other. Slowly feeling as my foot touched the ground, first the ball of my foot, then the heel followed, right foot, left foot. Feeling the warmth and light of the sun on my face, with the breeze gently caressing my hair. I was feeling so intensely that I was not thinking. My mind, usually a whirling of ping-ponging thoughts, was not racing at all. It was still. I admired the forest and could hear our steps on the ground, the dirt moving, the birds chirping, a very loud woodpecker. It was like everything was heightened, and as opposed to feeling bored, I was amazed by the beauty around me.

As I walked and was fully present in the now, I heard a voice. It was neither male nor female. I turned around to see if someone was actually speaking to me, but the voice came within my ear. It said, "Danusia's parents need her more than her children do now. She needs to go stay with her parents for a while." Danusia is my oldest and dearest friend, the one I did the Cher workouts with.

Strange that I would hear this out of the blue. I noted this and kept walking. Later, I learned that her mom was taking a downturn in health.

Then I heard: "Do you have anything to ask?"

Under normal circumstances, where I was not stilled, totally calmed and present, I would have reacted with disbelief or criticism. Actually, I would not have heard the voice in the first place.

Now, it seemed perfectly normal. "Yes, of course," I answered silently.

I then proceeded to have a conversation with my Self or Higher Self or the "Force." It felt like Neale Donald Walsch's book *Conversations with God*. I would ask a question and immediately, I would receive an answer.

I asked about my family, in particular, my girls, who were seven and nine at the time. The voice said, "They are fine. Remember they are your teachers, not the other way around."

I asked about my career and business, and the voice said, "Take one step at a time. The next step will be revealed. Your mind is twenty steps ahead of where you are in space and time, so you are getting tripped up."

On and on our conversation went. I asked questions for my husband, my sister, my friends. It was fast, and I felt like I could not have come up with those answers myself so quickly.

I am not sure how long my Q&A went on for, but it broke when my teachers stopped the group in a field by the retreat center and gave quiet verbal instructions on what was next on our itinerary.

"Nothing in all creation is so like God as silence."
– PATAÑJALI, THE YOGA SUTRAS OF PATAÑJALI

Why do I share this story? It is my own proof that there is more to this 3D reality that we live in. I believe there is so much more that we are not taught or ever exposed to. In fact, I think it is purposely hidden from us, as we would be too powerful otherwise. But herein lies the message of this chapter; we cannot only tap into this Force or Source when adversity strikes, we can live or aim to live connected to Source, surrender to it, stop worrying or trying to force things, and Be.

The goal in this lesson is to share with you my final but perhaps most potent secret to greater resilience. It is faith—having faith in something omnipotent, in a force larger than us, a universal loving energy, a divine intelligence that allows us to rise above the difficult situation at hand and view it from a higher/larger perspective; one not limited to this 3D life at this moment in time.

The goal is also to bring attention to the fact that spirituality has been found to be a significant contributor to resilience. My hope in this chapter is to also spark your interest in your own faith and spirituality and explore how it may enhance your personal strength in times of turmoil.

By this point, we do not have to revisit the concept of resilience. But let's recall that having resilience is like having shock absorbers so the bumps in the road are not as bumpy. The road is smoother, and you can glide over the bumps as opposed to be shaken by them if you can reframe an adversity from a larger perspective.

Let me explain. According to recent research published in the *Journal of Religion and Health,* in times of distress "religious people" have coping strategies, specifically what the researchers call "reappraisal" and "coping self-efficacy."

First let's tackle reappraisal. The researchers stated: "It has been suggested that religious practices could facilitate the use of reappraisal, by promoting reframing of negative cognitions to alter emotional states."

According to Berkeley Well-Being Institute: "Reappraisal involves cognitively reframing an event to reduce the negative emotions you feel."

I recall when a friend, just shy of her fortieth birthday, a most beautiful, loving soul with two young girls ages six and nine, the same age incidentally as my girls at the time, died tragically. All our hearts broke that day, never to be mended fully. I recall a mutual friend called to share the news, and I actually dropped to the floor when I heard. Although we all knew she was sick, we did not believe she could die. How was this possible? It was like someone came behind my knees and pushed them forward and I fell to the ground. I lay on my floor crying for three days. I do not know how her husband remained standing. But on the third day, something happened. I had a dream of her walking with me, as we used to, on the streets behind our homes. She looked healthier and happier than ever. She was dressed in a vibrant, frilly dress. As we walked, she ate the biggest cookie I ever saw. "The food in heaven tastes amazing," she said with a big smile on her angelic face. She looked and felt radiant and said, "All is as it should be, and I am still here. Just close your eyes and feel me."

After that dream, I was able to reframe the gut-wrenching situation. Although my heart still ached, I did not spend the day on the floor weeping. I felt like maybe, despite the raw pain I felt for her family, maybe God/Source had a greater plan. I could not, no matter how hard I tried, change this situation, but like the Serenity Prayer advocates, I could accept it a little more.

The second conclusion the researchers arrived at was that spiritually inclined individuals have "coping self-efficacy." What that means is that when things aren't going well for them or they are having problems, they have a confidence that they can get through it. My interpretation is they feel they are not alone with the problem; they feel supported by Source.

The really fascinating part of the study is the outcome of the reappraisal and coping self-efficacy. The researchers found that "Habitual engagement of reappraisal and high levels of perceived coping abilities, as fostered by religious coping, results in more adaptive behaviors that **promote increased resilience, reduce symptoms of distress, and maintain emotional well-being**." The bolds are mine.

This is just one study, but there are countless others that suggest that spirituality is not only linked to better coping skills in difficult situations (a.k.a. resilience), but also it is positively correlated with decreased stress, burnout, and greater feelings of well-being in general.

FOUR STRATEGIES TO STRENGTHEN YOUR SPIRITUALITY

If you are not sure where to start, here are four strategies to play with to strengthen your spiritual muscles:

1. Change in perspective

Recall that the researchers in the "Religiosity and Resilience" study found that reappraisal or cognitively reframing a distressing event can alter negative emotions.

One way to do that is to shift your awareness from being a victim to an observer.

In the book *Owner/Victim Choice*, the authors point out that when something "bad happens," victims often ask the question "Why me?" They shift the blame to others and believe things happen "to them." They do not take responsibility. They are powerless as they view themselves as victims of circumstance.

Next time something seemingly bad happens, notice how you respond. Or take a moment now to think back over some recent scenarios. If you see yourself as responding to difficult situations with victim-type behavior, know that you can rescript this thought process.

In the book, the authors suggest making the choice to become the owner of the situation. I like this a lot. It is about taking responsibility for whatever transpired, even if you did little to cause it. You are then empowered to do something about it. To act as opposed to react. It is a powerful state of mind and stance in life. But what if we could take this one step further and take a spiritual perspective? What if we could rise above the difficult circumstance and become an observer?

What does that even mean? I see it as floating up out of your body, out of the situation, higher and higher like a balloon until you are detached emotionally from the scenario and can watch it the way you would a movie. Once you can take this perspective of observer, you could then ask yourself if it is happening FOR you as opposed TO you.

It's a hard pill to swallow. What if everything that happens good or bad is for me? I recall losing a friend over a misunderstanding, a miscommunication really. It was heart-wrenching to feel so misinterpreted. It was so much easier to think she was irrational, and that somehow her trauma was triggered by the situation and she took it out on poor innocent me.

Did I mention, it is so much easier for the ego to be the victim? But if I rise above my ego and view this same circumstance with my friend as something that happened "for me," specifically that I somehow drew it to myself on some quantum energetic level, then a different story and energy unfolds. I see my own behavior, I see my own trauma, I see my patterns, and suddenly I feel forgiveness. And the anger dissipates, as do the old patterns of behavior. I also see that maybe we weren't actually the best of friends. I didn't feel like I could be authentically myself with her.

Observing takes quiet contemplation and a taming of the ego, which wants to be "right" as opposed to happy. By processing life and its daily circumstances from a consciousness, we see that we are all connected and there are no accidents. Suddenly the a-hole is there for you. They exist almost like a hologram. That doesn't mean you take their shit. The situation may be presenting itself so you learn how not to take it with grace.

This can be a whole book onto itself, but the key practice is to rise above our 3D experiences with their difficulties and see our life and situations from a higher, larger, and more universal perspective.

What if everything seemingly bad that happened, you asked yourself:

- How is this happening FOR me not to me?
- How is this difficulty a blessing?

2. Focus on what you can control—surrender the rest

In university on my computer screen I had the words "*Let Go and Let God*" written. Anytime my computer went into sleep mode, the phrase would show up and bounce around the screen in funny patterns. This happened for years! Whenever I returned to my room or rebooted my computer or stopped working, I would see this phrase over and over again. It reminded me in those super anxious moments, especially when studying for an exam or completing some project, that I could do the work and surrender. It honestly kept me sane.

I spoke about surrendering to Source earlier on in the book. Specifically, when I referred to the yogic practice of Isvara Pranidhana, pronounced as ish-va-ra-pra-nid-hah-na. I like saying it. My teachers spoke about it frequently. It is the last of the Niyamas of the Yoga Sutra, the main text of yoga.

This Sanskrit term is made up of two words: *Isvara*, which translates to "Higher Source" or the Divine, and *Pranidhana,* which means surrendering (sometimes it is translated to mean fixing). My teachers taught that Isvara Pranidhana invites us to surrender whatever transpires, good or bad, to the Highest Source. In essence, they taught it means cultivating a trusting relationship with the universe and everything around us. It means your mind or ego is no longer running the show—something greater, more intelligent, and infinite is.

The concept, as I interpret or understand it, is that when we truly surrender to our current reality, even when it sucks, we will receive wisdom and guidance from the universe, a higher self, or God/Source.

When I first really contemplated surrendering, it felt like giving up, but now I understand it to be one of the hardest yoga practices. I don't know about you, but although I deny it, I like to control things or at least feel I am in control of things in my life. Letting go is not at all easy—it's really hard.

Surrendering entails still doing your work and then offering it up. My teachers said Isvara Pranidhana is also translated as "offering the fruits of one's actions to the Divine." Or making everything we do an offering to something bigger than us. Imagine doing your work in such a way that it is worthy to be offered to the Divine. Imagine then letting the Divine sort out what best to do with it.

To me, a naturally inclined worrier, Isvara Prandihana is also a way to stop my mind from ruminating on potentially negative things that have not actually happened. When I find myself on this hamster wheel of worry, I turn and offer it up to Source. I surrender whatever it is I am obsessing about to the Highest. I *Let Go and Let God."*

This week, if you find yourself worrying or being anxious about a difficult situation, can you offer it up to the Divine? When struggling or worrying, I will say over and over, "Source, you take over." I actually say Jesus or Angels. It feels right, as I was brought up in the Christian faith. You can say Allah, Buddha, Divine, Gaia . . . whatever resonates.

3. Explore Ho'oponopono

Ho'oponopono is an ancient Hawaiian (kahuna) spiritual technology that means "To make right; to rectify an error." It is pronounced: Ho-oh-po-no-po-no. Again, fun to say. I was introduced to the practice about six years ago when I went to do a past-life regression with a most amazing hypnotherapist. She shared a story of a clinical psychologist Dr. Hew Len who healed a group of psychiatric patients without ever meeting with them. He strangely did this by holding the patients' files, feeling what came up for him as he thought of the crimes they had committed, taking responsibility for the feelings that arose, and repeating the mantra: "I'm sorry. Please forgive me. Thank you. I love you."

My analytical critical mind reacted with a "that's impossible," and to be honest, I dismissed the technique. Why was he taking responsibility and apologizing for them? I thought.

About two years ago, my friend Danusia shared a course with me she was taking that was offered by Joe Vitale, who I knew from watching the movie *The Secret*, and Dr. Len, the very psychologist who healed those psychiatric patients. Now, I was intrigued. Did this therapist actually cure the patients without ever seeing them? What did he do precisely? Why did he apologize to them when he had never met them? I decided to listen, and after about ten minutes, I was totally sucked into this eight-part program. I listened to every lesson several times. I could not comprehend how this technique worked, but I started to apply it in my life, and it felt good.

What I learned from the course:

Ho'oponopono is a "process that allows for the release of problems and blocks that cause stress, imbalance, and dis-ease within the SELF." It is not about the other person or external situation. The problem is not with the "patients" or the person on the street who cut you off, or your spouse, your parent, your kids, the toxic colleague at work, the traffic, etc.—it is about YOU. It is about taking 100 percent responsibility for the emotion that the situation brings up in you and clearing it by offering it to the Divine and repeating those four mantras.

It somehow feels like a combo of the first two strategies we discussed, doesn't it?

In the course, Dr. Len also said the technique is about forgiveness and freedom from toxic memories that replay in our subconscious minds. He said that our purpose or goal in life is to free ourselves of these toxic memories and restore our minds to a clean state or "zero point." He said that this is what all ancient masters did to become enlightened. We get to zero point by "cleaning," as Dr. Len calls it. It's specifically giving the Divine permission to transmute the negative thought, feeling, or emotion by repeating "I am sorry. Please forgive me. Thank you. I love you," over and over again.

If nothing else, imagine if we took more responsibility and said, "Thank you" and "I love you" more often.

This week, perhaps you can try it and see what happens.

4. Silence/Stillness

Herman Melville, the famous nineteenth century author of *Moby Dick* said, "Silence is the only Voice of God." I started this chapter on silence, so it seemed appropriate to finish it on silence as well.

Silence is a beautiful and basic spiritual practice that we all have access to. I think of it as a counterbalance to the very loud world we live in. Just on a physical level, the constant noise, music, podcasts, beeps, and dings are stressors to our nervous system. The noise also cuts us off from the whispers of our soul. It is no coincidence that all the gurus, monks, and spiritual teachers spent time in silence.

Wayne Dyer, in *A Spiritual Solution to Every Problem*, writes, **"Communing quietly with the spiritual force is our way of becoming one with it."** According to Dyer, being in silence, we can communicate and become one with the Source. Beautiful, isn't it?

To me, it is not just about being silent, it is also about stilling the mind. This is actually the essence of yoga. In the Yoga Sutras, an ancient guide often referred to as the "basis of yoga philosophy," Patañjali, the author, defined yoga as "citta vritti nirodha." This literally means that if you still the activity of the mind, you are in yoga. Interesting, as here in the West, we often think yoga is about exercise or flexibility. "Yogas citta vritti nirodhah" translates to "yoga is the stilling or controlling of the modifications or fluctuations of the mind." *Yogas* means to join or unite, *chitta* refers to the mind or consciousness, *vritti* translates to fluctuations or modifications, and *nirodha* means quieting of or controlling.

So, yoga, according to Patañjali, is a process to retrain the vrittis/fluctuations of the mind. My teachers said it is like calming the surface of a choppy body of water so that we can see all the way to the bottom. When we see the bottom, we find the "True Self."

Let's circle this back to resilience. According to Patañjali, we suffer not necessarily because bad things happen but because of this unstill mind and the "kleshas." Apologies for throwing all these Sanskrit words at you. The kleshas are obstacles or afflictions that arise in the mind. I have heard them referred to as mental poisons. They are thoughts that skew our perception of life and generate suffering in our experience. Namely, they do this by making us imagine that we are separate from others and from the universe. They also keep us in a state of fear, which according to the *Course in Miracles* (another good spiritual text) is the opposite of love. The five kleshas in the Yoga Sutra are Avidya (ignorance), Asmita (egoism), Raga (attachment), Dvesa (repulsion and aversion), and Abhinivesha (fear of death and the will to live).

The key here is not to know the fancy Sanskrit terms but to note that a lot, if not most, of our suffering is in the mind. It reminds me of that quote we have all heard by John Milton: "The mind is its own place, and in itself can make a heaven of hell, a hell of heaven."

We, therefore, have the power to handle practically any difficult situation with more comfort and ease by engaging in practices and creating habits that still our mind and tame our kleshas, practices that put us in touch with our true selves. These include but are not limited to yoga, meditation, pranayama, silence, prayer, quiet contemplation, journaling, and even spending time in nature. These practices connect us with something both deep within and that "Force" that is deep without. It takes commitment, discipline, and a strong WHY, but I can tell you just from personal experience that when you start on this journey, you will suddenly find yourself in your heart more and sometimes unexpectedly feel joy for no reason at all. So that brings us to the end of the strategies to connect to your spiritual essence.

Recall that spiritually inclined individuals have the ability to reframe difficult situations and "coping self-efficacy," i.e., they feel they can get through whatever life throws at them. In a word, one can call them resilient.

Changing our perspectives from being victims to observers, surrendering to a Higher Source, forgiving, being grateful through a practice like Ho'oponopono, and stilling our minds are just a few strategies that allow us to connect on a deeper level to our innate spiritual self.

Now it's time to Do the Work and BE Resilient

THE EXPLORE YOUR SPIRITUALITY CHALLENGE

What practices listed here are you drawn to that still your mind and bring you peace and joy?

1. Change in perspective—asking how is this happening *for* me?

2. Surrender to the Highest.

3. Explore Ho'oponopono.

4. Embrace Silence.

Choose ONE practice that you can do daily. It can be as simple as putting your hand on your heart in the morning and saying, "Thank you, Source, for another day," or carving out ten minutes of just pure silence.

The last word on spirituality and resilience:
Enhancing your spiritual life is a way to bolster your capacity to handle difficult situations. It is also positively correlated with decreased stress, burnout, and greater feelings of well-being in general.

"Every morning put your mind into your heart and stand in the presence of God all the day long."
– PATAÑJALI, THE YOGA SUTRAS OF PATAÑJALI

PART THREE.
THE JOURNEY CONTINUES

CONCLUSION

"You are the creator of your own destiny."
—Swami Vivekananda

As a long-term student and practitioner of yoga therapy, I encountered the concept of "sva tantram." *Sva* means self and *tantram* means reliance. In my yoga therapist training program, we learned that as therapists, we are to guide the individual student to a complete state of self-reliance or total independence.

Although this book is not about yoga therapy, the concept remains. I hope that I have guided you through the theory and practices that will enhance your personal resilience. Now it is up to you to create space, enough silence to tap into your inner wisdom, and self-determination to keep going.

There is something very powerful about being fully established in oneself. To be grounded in the practices that serve you best and make you stronger, more energized, present, and alive.

Society has taught us to look externally to find joy, peace, happiness, and reassurance, as well as to end our suffering. What if you can be the person in your life to do that?

Please do not mistake my words here: If you or someone you know is suffering mentally, physically, or emotionally, I am not saying to not seek help. To ask for help is an act of courage.

What I am trying to convey is that through self-study, "svadyaya," and "sva tantram" self-reliance, you may suffer less and not have to get to the point where you need to seek support. May you find strength in yourself that you did not know existed. As the quote by Swami Vivekananda suggests, you have the power to create your destiny.

Part of that destiny creation is not focusing on our problems all the time but on our desired outcomes AND strengthening ourselves to the point that our problems become smaller and those bumps in the road less tumultuous.

Dr. NC, our yoga therapist teacher/guru from India, once drew two parallel lines on the board. One was large and one much smaller. He then said, "Often we feel that our problems are the big line towering over us. We feel like we are the small line and can't handle the problem."

He encouraged us not to focus constantly on the problem where our mind wants to go but to bring our focus to getting stronger through practices like those I presented in this book. Over time, as you become stronger by creating habits out of the practices, something miraculous happens—you become the big line and the problem becomes the smaller line. As the big line, you have the energy and mindset to handle the issue. Of course, this is metaphorical, but it comes back to the idea we started the book with, that we live in uncertain times. There is constant change and volatility, bad news, competition, and chaos. If we get sucked into focusing on these problems, we are done, our central nervous system is shot, we flip our lids, and we become depressed and anxious.

Instead, if we move our focus away from the problems and focus on:

- improving our sleep
- eating high-vibrational foods consciously
- moving our bodies
- breathing deeply and fully
- becoming present
- generating positivity and laughing often
- connecting with heart and authenticity
- creating boundaries to recharge
- living with full intention
- communing with Spirit . . .

. . . we become centered, energized, and dare I say, happy, and strong.

Recall "what you practice grows stronger," so practice being the best you that you can imagine. And that reminds me, don't forget to use your imagination. Visualize that you are strong, that you are living in a blissful state, that you are already who you want to be. Dr. NC said, "If you act like a fish searching for water, you will never find it. Instead, know you are already there."

It's a new way to be. Know that you are resilient. Breathe joy and strength into your body daily and repeat to yourself with a smile on your face: "I am happy, healthy, strong, and present. I AM RESILIENT."

And so, it is!

ACKNOWLEDGMENTS

Just like it takes a village to raise a child, it seems the same is true to write and publish a book.

Thank you for the encouragement, patience, and support from Sabrina, Kelly, and the whole Soul Seed Legacy House publishing team.

Thank you to my daughters who are my first priority in the world. Everything else just finds its place. They are also my mirror, my teachers, and my greatest loves.

Thank you again to my husband, Aubrey, for his never-ending support and countless hours spent helping me to create the Resilient by Design program. This book wouldn't exist without it.

Thank you to my parents, especially my mother who seems to think I can do anything I put my mind to.

Thank you to my friend Danusia who I have referred to multiple times in this book. Our friendship has been one of my greatest blessings and is a resilience-enhancing secret sauce.

Thank you to my creative and literary friend Jelena for her enthusiasm, ideas, and feedback.

Thank you to Michele for her beautiful input on the mindfulness section of our program. Her ideas and meditations are reflected in the book.

Thank you to Rita who co-instructs on our programs. Her insights and thoughtfulness help the programs and therefore the content evolve.

Thank you to my yoga teachers at Yoga Therapy Toronto for their inspiration and embodied wisdom.

Finally, thank you to YOU, the reader. I had an image of you in my mind as I wrote this book. I imagined you struggling, stressed, and overwhelmed by the chaotic world we live in and yet searching for another way. I humbly hope that maybe just ONE thing inspired you to create your new happier, healthier, more resilient way to be in the world.

I send you all my love and light.

Monica

RESOURCES
(IN ALPHABETICAL ORDER)

BOOKS

The 5 AM Club, Robin S. Sharma (2018)

The 7 Habits of Highly Effective People, Stephen R. Covey (1989)

A Course in Miracles, Helen Schucman (1976)

Better Than Before, Gretchen Rubin (2015)

Comfortable with Uncertainty, Pema Chödrön (2003)

Conversations with God, Neale Donald Walsch (1995)

Dodging Energy Vampires, Christiane Northrup (2018)

Emotional Intelligence, Daniel Goleman (2005)

Feel the Fear and Do It Anyway, Susan Jeffers (1987)

First Things First, Stephen R. Covey (1999)

The Four Agreements, Don Miguel Ruiz (1997)

The Four Tendencies, Gretchen Rubin (2017)

How to Train a Wild Elephant, Jan Chozen Bays (2011)

In the Sphere of Silence, Vijay Eswaran (2005)

The Joy Diet, Martha Beck (2003)

The ONE Thing, Gary Keller (2013)

The Owner/Victim Choice, Dennis R. Deaton and Steven L. Bodhaine (2002)

Pandora's Lunchbox, Melanie Warner (2014)

The Power of Now, Eckhart Tolle (1997)

The Power of Positive Thinking, Norman Vincent Peale (1952)

Principles and Practice of YOGA THERAPY, Dr. N. Chandrasekaran (2012)

The Stress Solution, Dr. Rangan Chatterjee (2019)

There's a Spiritual Solution to Every Problem, Wayne W. Dyer (1975)

Think and Grow Rich, Napoleon Hill (1937)

What You Want Wants You, Suzanne Eder (2023)

The Whole-Brain Child, Daniel J. Siegel and Tina Payne Bryson (2011)

The Yoga of Breath, Richard Rosen (2002)

You Can Heal Your Life, Louise Hay (1984)

WEBSITES

https://academic.oup.com/ajcn/article/101/6/1251/4626878/

https://academic.oup.com/eurheartj/

https://academic.oup.com/scan/article/10/12/1758/2502572?login=false/

https://ajcn.nutrition.org/content/early/2015/05/06/ajcn.114.100925.abstract/

https://amanet.org/

https://apa.org/

https://assets.fellowes.com/press/181018-UK-sedentary-research.pdf/

https://bbc.com/news/

https://bbk.ac.uk/news/good-quality-me-time-vital-for-home-and-work-well-being/

https://becomingminimalist.com/

https://berkeleywellbeing.com/reappraisal.html/

https://blog.biotrust.com/afterburn-effect-epoc-exercises/

https://brendon.com/

https://brenebrown.com/

https://canr.msu.edu/news/
exercise_at_work_is_it_possible_and_what_are_the_benefits/

https://ccare.stanford.edu/uncategorized/
connectedness-health-the-science-of-social-connection-infographic/

https://centreformindfulleadership.com/

https://chopra.com/articles/
learn-the-ujjayi-breath-an-ancient-yogic-breathing-technique/

https://cytowic.net/

https://dailyshoring.com/neurons-that-fire-together-wire-together/

https://drdansiegel.com/hand-model-of-the-brain/

https://drhyman.com/blog/2022/02/03/podcast-ep490/

https://drjoedispenza.com/

https://drshaunashapiro.com/

https://emmaseppala.com/

https://exploringyourmind.com/
belonging-to-a-social-group-improves-your-health-and-happiness

https://fastcompany.com/52717/change-or-die/

https://forbes.com/sites/priceonomics/2018/07/10/heres-how-much-
money-do-you-save-by-cooking-at-home/?sh=12f12a2d35e5/

https://gallup.com/workplace/236561/employees-strengths-outper-
form-don.aspx/

https://hammernutrition.com/blogs/
endurance-news-weekly/146-reasons-sugar-ruins-your-health/

https://hbr.org/2016/06/
resilience-is-about-how-you-recharge-not-how-you-endure/

https://health.harvard.edu/blog/mindfulness-meditation-helps-fight-insomnia-improves-sleep-201502187726/

https://health.harvard.edu/mind-and-mood/relaxation-techniques-breath-control-helps-quell-errant-stress-response/

https://hse.ru/data/2011/06/28/1216307711/Gazzaniga.%20The%20Cognitive%20Neurosciences.pdf/

https://integrativenutrition.com/

https://jhu.edu/

https://jimrohn.com/

https://jonkabat-zinn.com/

https://journals.lww.com/psychosomaticmedicine/Abstract/2000/09000/Exercise_Treatment_for_Major_Depression_.6.aspx/

https://journals.plos.org/plosmedicine/article?id=10.1371/journal.pmed.1000316/

https://julianneholtlunstad.com/

https://leadershipwellness.ca/

https://lifehacker.com/jerry-seinfelds-productivity-secret-281626/

https://link.springer.com/article/10.1007/s10943-020-01160-y/

https://maryengelbreit.com/

https://mayoclinic.org/healthy-lifestyle/adult-health/expert-answers/sitting/faq-20058005/

https://medicaldaily.com/

https://mindworks.org/blog/physical-mental-benefits-of-meditation/

https://ncbi.nlm.nih.gov/pmc/articles/PMC5919946/

https://nytimes.com/

https://observer.com/2016/08/
this-is-the-best-way-to-motivate-yourself-to-exercise-4-proven-secrets/

https://oem.bmj.com/content/62/9/588/

https://ohsheglows.com/2010/11/23/vegan-mac-n-cheese/

https://positivepsychology.com/

https://pubmed.ncbi.nlm.nih.gov/

https://pursuit-of-happiness.org/history-of-happiness/
martin-seligman-psychology/

https://rickhanson.net/

https://science.howstuffworks.com/caffeine4.htm/

https://self-i-dentity-through-hooponopono.com/
morrnahs-questions-and-answers/

https://sjweh.fi/

https://sleep.hms.harvard.edu/

https://sleepinstitute.org/

https://telegraph.co.uk/science/2016/08/24/
having-no-friends-could-be-as-deadly-as-smoking-harvard-universi/

https://theartofcharm.com/entrepreneurship/
company-keep-determines/

https://thichnhathanhfoundation.org/

https://tonyrobbins.com/

https://ucl.ac.uk/news/2010/may/ucl-study-overtime-bad-your-heart

https://utoronto.ca/news/prevent-depression-walk-20-minutes-day/

https://yogapedia.com/

For additional resources, please use this QR code. It will direct you to my site where you'll find challenge exercises, assessments, bonuses, and additional learning material by topic to help you dive deeper into all the areas of resilience.

SOUL SEED
L E G A C Y · H O U S E

At Soul Seed Legacy House, we help thought leaders
and creative entrepreneurs capture their vision in the
form of nonfiction books, journals, workbooks,
affirmation cards, and personal growth products.

Our mission is to help our authors grow and scale a
platform far beyond the book, protect their soul's work,
and turn their message into a legacy!

www.sslegacyhouse.com

@sslegacyhouse

SOUL SEED
LEGACY · HOUSE